PRAGMATICS

OF

COMMUNITY

ORGANIZATION

3RD EDITION

Bill Lee M.S.W., ED.D.
McMaster University
School of Social Work

CommonAct Press
Mississauga, Ontario

COMMONACT PRESS
7050 Old Mill Lane
Mississauga, ON L5W 1A1
email: info@commonact.com
website: www.commonact.com

Canadian Cataloguing in Publication Data
LEE, BILL, 1942-

Pragmatics of community organization
3rd Edition 2nd Printing
Includes bibliographical referees.

ISBN 0-921159-05-6

1.   Community organization.

2.   Social action.

3.   Social service

4.   Community organization - Study and teaching.

5.   Social action - Study and teaching

6.   Social work education

I.   Title

HV41.L44 1993   361.8   C93-093147-5

Printed with Union Labour

Almost every significant social progress in our respective countries starts out with one or two or three people saying, "something is wrong and we are going to make it right".

—Ralph Nader

To know what you prefer instead, of humbly saying "Amen" to what the world tells you you ought to prefer, is to have kept your soul alive.

—Robert Louis Stevenson

Good travels at a snail's pace. Those who want to do good are not selfish, they are not in a hurry, they know that to impregnate people with good requires a long time.

—Mohandas K. Gandhi

Our struggle as women, men, blacks, workers, Brazilians, North American, French, or Bolivians, is influenced by our gender, race, class, culture, and history - conditionings that mark us. Our struggle, nevertheless, departs from these conditionings and converges in the direction of being more in the direction of universal objectives. Or else, for me at least, the fight would make no sense.

—Paolo Freire

This book is dedicated to my daughter,
Mary Josephine Lee
(July 24, 1967 - May 6, 1994).

She always understood the need for struggle
no matter what the odds,
in her own life and in fighting for
other people and the environment.

Foreword

This text book is very familiar to me. I have used it as the required text for my community practice courses for over ten years now - indeed since the very first edition; which came out in paperback form, with a binding that broke apart when you opened it. The breaking actually served a useful purpose for photocopying, which I thought might be the intent of Bill, since he is so concerned with the sharing of information - which is, as he notes, a source of power.

Since that time, I have challenged Bill to answer a particularly important question: "Do you believe what you write?". For an Aboriginal person, like myself, I was: a) actually testing his character; b) determining whether the source of his knowledge was rooted in common people (who are residents of the communities); and c) whether his character was consistent with the sentiment of his words. It was important for me because, like many other people, I have come across so many academics who publish for the sake of publishing; who have usurped the knowledge of the people for their own aggrandizement and promotion; or whose work was not discernible in practice. One of the reasons for asking these questions was the following: I was going to ask him to work with me in a very delicate situation - involving a First Nation community which was asking for some help with evolving into a better functioning reality. We would be given the opportunity to put ideas into practice and, as Freire would say: "...to make intellectuals meaningful to the common people".

So Bill passed the test - the Indian test. And so has the content of his books.

The outstanding feature of this text is its rootedness in the *real* situation, and the dynamics of the people. It gives solid advice to the practitioner on how to be human in a human context; how to be respectful of people in their intimate context, which is their community; how to read situations in which people find themselves while interfacing with institutions (and the people who work in them). All of this is done so that a positive outcome can occur, in spite of the power difference that exists in this scenario: to show how to struggle without unnecessarily making enemies but, importantly, without maintaining a powerless situation; how people can learn to assess their own situation and its political, social, and economic dimensions; and how they can create strategies from this information, and then mobilize into action in an informed way.

As an Aboriginal person, I am pleased that Bill acknowledges the spiritual realm in this edition of the text - it is an important part of the make-up of the community. To change a community is a conscious choice which shows itself in the way people experience the spirit of the community, and of themselves. Empowerment, by people, of themselves results more in the tangible sense of spirituality they possess and not the material change that occurs. I get this from this book, and I get it from practice which I gather from this book.

It is not uncommon for students who have taken my course in community practice to come back, after they leave, and tell me that this text has helped them in their practice. They indicate that the contents enabled them to:
- organize an apparent chaotic and unfamiliar context into which they had been inserted or assigned;
- focus on the empowerment intent of community social change;
- understand their role within the context - especially that the definition of the problem, the dynamics, and the desired outcome belong to the people who are there;
- understand the relationships between people in power, the source of that power, and the community people who wish to influence it;
- feel confident and unconfused by diverse situations.

The book has real and lasting benefit: high praise for any textbook.

Mac Saulis
Ottawa
September, 1998

INTRODUCTION TO THE THIRD EDITION

Initially when we published the first edition of *Pragmatics of Community Organization*, it was to fill what we thought was a significant need within a fairly small population: a coherent, practical guide to thinking about the practice of working with communities, for community work teachers and students. It has turned out that it is being used by students, teachers, beginning workers and activists in a whole variety of community settings in Canada and the U.S., as well as in countries outside North America. It was also nice to discover that activists and "old hands" were finding it useful.

The focus of the first edition was on the so-called phases and political nature of community organizing. In the second edition I added a framework to assist us in thinking about what we were trying to achieve - the objectives of our work. This third edition, I hope, will take us deeper into both areas. A chapter has been added on roles and skills required by workers, as well as a section which offers a clearer conception of the place and character of community - particularly its political character. There is also discussion of the terrain of opposition, and a range of material has been injected throughout the book that tries to address our ability to think about strategy and tactics. We have attempted to make the book more user friendly - introducing more summary charts, diagrams and pictures. Readers will also note that the bibliography has been expanded and updated to reflect the interesting material that has appeared in the last seven years. There are recommendations regarding useful additional readings accompanying most chapters, for those who wish to explore the ideas and notions discussed in the work more deeply. Finally, I have been able to do what I love to do most - work and talk with community workers, teachers and activists. With their assistance we have been able to add to the number of examples and bring in new ones, which reflect and highlight the contemporary context and struggle. As well, these conversations have helped me maintain my sense of hope in these troubled times. Indeed, many of the quotes found throughout the text are reflections of the importance, and reality, of what community work can engender.

What I hope this new edition will do, then, is to maintain and strengthen the focus on community organizing as a coherent, political practice anchored within a context of specific outcomes. This book is written for the same population as the first: students and teachers of community work in colleges and universities, beginning practitioners and community activists. I hope that the new material is useful in provoking thought about how and why we do community development.

As with the first two editions of Pragmatics, this book owes its existence to a number of people, and when I start to thank them I fear and know that I will forget some. Nevertheless, I feel that I resist the temptation to merely thank people en masse and hope everyone will get the message.

First, I very much appreciate the Foreword written by Mac Saulis, who has been a friend as well as a challenging colleague. My wife Cecelia read and reread chunks of the manuscript, and gave me valuable editorial comments, as well as a lot of encouragement. Mike Balkwill encouraged and badgered me to "get the damned thing done". CommonAct's Marney Cuff's creative editorial work, not to mention her encouragement, is evident in the final shape and look of the book. There are some people within the First Nations struggle that have indirectly provided this book with a valuable grass roots perspective: Barb Nahwegahbow, Rene Masching, Harry and Eva Sock and Sheri Pictou.

A number of my colleagues at McMaster University, particularly Jim Rice and Sheila Sammon, have encouraged the community development approach to social work. I also wish to thank Sue Watt for helping me get to Nigeria. My three colleagues from the community work group - Susan McGrath, Ken Moffat (York University) and Usha George (University of Toronto) - have provided me with important insights, particularly around the importance of citizenship.

There have been many community organizers and activists who have shared their experiences with me and let me share mine with them, particularly Louise Martin in New Orleans, Pat McNaughton in Nicaragua, Janet Fishlock at AHAA and now in Ghana. I especially wish to thank Marion Porter in Cork, Ireland, and Shannon Beard in

Toronto, who opened my eyes to the great strength and energy of those fighting against disability discrimination. Also, there are many individuals who helped me through the maze of statistics and material used throughout this text: Suzanne Brown at the Social Planning and Research Council (Hamilton, Ontario); the staff and community support network of David Christopherson NDP MPP (Hamilton Centre); and the staff of Bryan Prince Bookseller, Hamilton.

Finally, and most importantly, the members of various communities, particularly the women of Banamwandu Tumelin'dde Co-operative Group in Uganda; the community research team at Jos University in Nigeria; members of the Affordable Housing Action Association in Mississauga; the workers and staff at the Chetwynd Project in Toronto; the workers of the Children's Aid Society of Toronto's Community Work Program; and the First Nations people of Big Cove (New Brunswick), Toronto and Hamilton, who have allowed me into their lives to learn along with them. In many ways, to me, this seems like a collective project.

Bill Lee
Toronto, Ontario
August 1998

Design and Layout by: Sandra Clarke, Blue Moon Creative (Hamilton)
Cover designs by: Chandra L. Rice
Cover photos by: A/C Van Gemerden (Hamilton)
Illustrations by: M.J. Lee, J. M. Lee, A. Martin, and T. Bella
Photos by: C. Lee, M. Balkwill, B. Lee, J. Fishlock, and Affordable
Housing Action Association (AHAA)

A NOTE ON THE USE OF THIS BOOK

In this book, the process of assisting communities with change is divided into two sections. The first deals with the broad strokes of community organizing - context, objectives, and roles and skills. The second covers the more detailed "how" we go about our work. It is broken down into phases that appear in sequence, and are more or less discreet (see Figure II, Section II, p.70). This is a bit ideal, however; I do not wish to suggest that each phase represents a bunch of tasks that, once done, will set up the next phase perfectly. The phases are meant to represent clusters of issues that need to be dealt with in the work of community organization. Though there is a general and logical sequence to when these issues need to be addressed, the phases will often overlap in your own experience in working with a community of people. Things, of course, will not be so ordered and logical. Thus, when you are using this book in practice, feel free to skip around according to the needs of your situation. It would be a good idea to give the book a quick initial read, to get a sense of what is in it and where things are - then use as your requirements dictate.

A NOTE ON PRONOUNS

As you peruse this tome, you will note that the masculine and feminine personal pronouns - he and she, her and him, hers and his - are used alternately to refer to the community worker. This is not the result of an inattentive editor - it has been done consciously in an effort to avoid gender bias of language, as well as to reflect the reality that many organizers and important actors within communities are women.

CONTENTS

TABLE OF FIGURES

1-1 Distribution of Household Incomes
1-2 The Structuring of Self-efficacy
1-3 Relationships and Outcomes of a Positive Self-image
1-4 Relationships and Outcomes of a Negative Self-image
1-5 Levels of Relationships in Society
1-6 Bureaucratic Organization Model
1-7 Conceptualizing the Pragmatic Approach

2-1 Integration of Empowerment and Community Organizing Objectives
2-2 Dimensions of Community Organizing

II: Phases of Community Organizing

4-1 Pre-entry Summary

5-1 Contact and Engagement Summary

6-1 Action/Refection Spiral
6-2 Community Analysis Summary

7-1 Activity/Level of Member Commitment
7-2 Organization Development Summary

8-1 Levels of Support and Opposition
8-2 Popular Action Summary

AN INTRODUCTION TO COMMUNITY ORGANIZING[1]
An Historical Perspective

Community organization - the purposeful bringing together of people and structuring their effort to achieve some alteration or development in the life of a group - is usually thought of as a modern intervention a creation of the "activist" and "idealistic" 1960's (Biklen, 1983). In reality, however, it has probably existed for as long as recorded history. While not in the running for the title of the world's oldest profession, there is ample evidence of its antiquity, of people taking responsibility for solving local problems or challenging unjust social conditions. It is easy to identify examples of its practice throughout the history of most societies.

The Old Testament tells how Moses and his brother, Aaron, organized one of the first recorded non-violent revolutions in history. Enslaved for generations by the Egyptians, the Israelites banded together and began their great exodus out of oppression. Centuries later, Saul of Tarsus (St. Paul) organized the first Christian communities into small, strong communities founded on principles of equality and sharing.

In medieval Italy, Francis of Assisi - after experiencing a deep spiritual conversion - recognized the poverty and corruption around him. Rejecting all class distinctions, he took to the road to organize religious communities dedicated to the relief of poverty, contemplation, and work for the poor. His efforts provided the impetus for a movement of religious orders that swept through all of Europe. (Boff, 1982)

In the 1700s in North America, the brilliant Shawnee organizer and leader Tecumseh emerged. In response to the long series of encroachments and violations of the advancing Euro-Americans (who were threatening the way of life of indigenous North Americans), he formed a powerful Confederacy of North American First Nations against the land-grabbing of the border states. (Berton, 1980: 52-69) Recognized by friend and enemy alike as a gifted orator and organizer, he is considered the forefather of the twentieth-century First Nations movements (Edmunds, 1984).

Before and during World War I, Sylvia Pankhurst was one of the most effective organizers of the Women's Suffrage Movement in England (Tremain, 1973). Inspired by a belief in socialism and a well-developed social conscience, she fought for women's rights, particularly among the poor in London's East End. She also helped to build strong and effective organizations for the poor and for peace. She believed that no society was just if any of its citizens were political or economic slaves. (Romero, 1987)

The late 1800s to mid 1900s witnessed, perhaps, the world's most remarkable organizer: Mohandas K. Gandhi. Through his work as an advocate for the rights of oppressed Indians, he gained his reputation as the father of Indian independence. Of greater importance, however, were his creative innovations in the philosophy and technology of non-violent resistance. (Brown, 1989; Gandhi, 1951) Gandhi believed not only that every individual should pursue truth and individual spiritual realization; but also that this could only be accomplished through interdependence and mutual responsibility. He maintained that the way to address injustice is to reconstruct socio-economic life, basing it on principles of truth and non-violence, which stress the interconnectedness and mutuality among all living things. (Brown, 1989)

From the late 1930s to the early 1970s, North America saw the abrasive organizing style of Saul D. Alinsky. Working in ghettos throughout the U.S., and in his training program in Chicago, Alinsky - with his emphasis on mass based organizations and confrontation - influenced organizing activity all over the continent. (Horwitt, 1989; Finks, 1984) He believed that freedom and equality do not come as gifts; they are acquired through struggle. If people join together, he felt, they can generate the power to make the changes necessary to live with dignity.

During roughly the same period, Dorothy Day worked and her colleagues[2] established the Catholic Workers Movement, a potent force for social change for poor people in the United States. A writer and activist, Day found in the Gospels an understanding of human liberation, and a sense of community and solidarity, much larger than traditional politics could provide. Her writings were frequently confrontational and contentious, and her actions always challenged the institutional forces which lead to poverty.

In the 1930s, Moses Coady emerged on the east coast of Canada as the Co-operative Movement took root and flourished. Believing that the capitalist system had failed the people, Coady struggled to convince people that through co-operative principles, community action, and planning, they could obtain economic stability and become masters of their own destiny. (Laidlaw, 1961) Before he died in 1959, he helped to set up many working-peoples' co-operative economic enterprises. The institute at St. Francis Xavier University in Antigonish, Nova Scotia (which bears his name) was set up to assist people from all over the world in learning the principles and techniques of co-operative development

From the 1960s until his death in 1997, Latin American adult educator Paulo Freire worked at developing the practice of conscientization (Freire, 1970). This approach to community development posits the ability and the necessity of the oppressed to develop a unique understanding of, and action for, their own situation. Freire believed strongly in the notion of praxis – action and reflection going hand in hand. His work and ideas have affected many community workers, particularly those working with the very poor in developing countries and throughout the world.

Founder of the United Farm Workers of America, Cesar Chavez (from the 1950s until his death in 1993) waged a non-violent battle against the environmental, political and economic exploitation caused by agricultural producers, local and state governments, the Teamsters Union, and mega corporations. Chavez, like Gandhi, attributed his perseverance in his commitments to his beliefs in non-violence, God and truth - which he believed was the ultimate way to work for social change.

In the 1960s George Manuel was one of the leading organizers in First Nations communities (McFarlane, 1993). Drawing on his experience growing up in residential schools (where he got and recovered from TB which left him with a serious disability) and living in Native settlements in British Columbia, he worked to develop local, provincial and finally national organizations that would fight for the rights of Aboriginal people. He was the first president of the National Indian Brotherhood, now called the Assembly of First Nations.

The convergence of the environmental crisis and the struggle of Indigenous Peoples in Latin America has produced the extraordinary organizer and leader, Paiakon.[3] Born in the mid 1950s in the Brazilian rain forest, he realized that the European civilization posed a serious threat to his people, the Kaiapo. At the age of fourteen he left his village to spend two years with a Portuguese missionary to learn the language and customs of the people invading the Kaiapo lands. He returned to lead a successful fight against a mining company that had devastated their territory. Subsequently, they established a new village deep in the rain forest. Paiakon has dedicated himself to bringing together the many nations of the Para and Mato Grosso states in Brazil. This Pan-Indian coalition works on resisting the logging, mining and hydro-electric interests that are devastating the physical environment and killing the First Nations people of the rain forest.

As these few examples suggest, community organization has been a basic function in society. Its work transcends divisions of history, gender, race, religion and national boundaries. First Nations, Labour, Black, and Women's movements, for example, have had many good organizers who developed communities that have made significant achievements.[4] Most community development workers have not attained the same high profile as the people above. Indeed, organizers who become well-known leaders are the exception. The role of the organizer in this kind of work is to develop leadership, as well as active people's organizations, that can exercise their ability to affect the social contexts in which they live. This is what community organization is most about – people realizing their citizenship, their right and ability to influence their environment, and taking responsibility for their lives. What is clear, however, is that those mentioned above, as well as the many unknown workers, are people who organized powerful communities able to affect the social contexts in which they live.

The Current Context of Practice

This new era in social policy reflects the increased power of the corporate sector and the influence of globalization. Governments no longer seem willing to insure conditions of citizenship implied in the social contract. They are no longer committed to full employment, unwilling to redistribute resources in ways that alter the structure of wealth, and are not prepared to create programs that protect citizens against the forces of the global economy.
—Jim Rice and Michael J. Prince (forthcoming 2000)

The questions and issues that this book attempts to examine are framed at a specific time, and within a particular set of social, political and economic conditions. The people mentioned above confronted the issues, and used the strategies and resources, of their own times. We live in a period in which principles of materialism, efficiency and the "bottom line" appear to rule. The rich are getting richer - paying less of their fair share of taxes and making obscene profits within an increasingly less regulated marketplace. Middle class folks are increasingly squeezed, and less secure in the lean and mean global economy. And the poor are getting poorer. This is not accidental, nor is it a short term trend that the "market will straighten out". This is a deliberate attack on notions of equity, citizenship and social responsibility. When we raise questions of fairness, equality and social justice we do so within a society dominated by neo-conservative ideology and propaganda - an ideology that seeks to have us accept a world safe for companies but dangerous for people. The response then is typically: "Yes, those are very laudable goals but we must be practical, and be thankful for what we have. There are global forces at work here". This makes for a problematic context for community work. Ours is a collectivist, egalitarian and process orientation; facing trends that are individualistic, elitist, material and inhumane. At the same time, it is these very individualistic and competitive notions that make community organization particularly relevant. The apparent triumphant economic philosophy of the "neo-cons" has had important and terrible implications for the vulnerable sectors of our populations, whether in Canada, the USA, Europe or any of the so called developing areas of the world. The movie, "Roger and Me" documented the complete callousness with which General Motors (in the 1980s) dumped 30,000 workers in its Flint (Michigan) plants and brought a thriving urban centre to its knees. Companies and governments continue to downsize, with the same lack of concern for workers. A community worker friend in Nicaragua said that "Since the Americans bought the election the bottom has dropped out of everything. You can see the Mercedes all over the place as the rich return from Miami. But you also can't avoid seeing the begging, prostitution and crime that have returned with them."

Community workers need to think about working in this context. This is not to suggest, however, that we should simply "lower our sights". Nor does this mean that being aware of the context necessarily leads us to understand why we "can't win". Focusing on the real material conditions in which we live can (and must) also lead us to ask questions that will point to analysis and action that is likely to be more successful, in terms of empowerment and the search for social justice.

Endnotes

[1] While we agree with Wharf (in Wharf and Clague 1997), that *community organization* is probably the most appropriate term, at this point other terms - *community development; social development; adult education; and community work* - are used; the variety actually reflects the state of the practice.

[2] The mystic and poet, Thomas Merton, and the great American social critic, Michael Harrington, both worked with Day.

[3] I am indebted to environmentalist/broadcaster Dr. David Suzuki, who is both a friend and co-worker of Paiakon, for providing me with the story of this remarkable individual.

[4] See *Indian Country* by Peter Matthiesson (1992); *Chief* by Roy MacGregor (1990); and *Feminist Organizing For Change* by Adamson, *et. al.*(1988), for discussions of some of the issues and personalities in these movements in North America.

GLOSSARY OF RELEVANT TERMS

One of the aims of this book is to keep things as simple and straightforward as possible. Sometimes, however, a form of technical language (or jargon) is unavoidable - either the issues or the topics are themselves complex, or no simple language that is available is adequate to express the precise meaning of what we want to talk about. What is offered here is a quick guide to the more technical terms that may not be in current use outside of community work. The glossary is placed at the beginning of our discussion so that it is apparent and easy to find. It may be useful to scan it before getting into the book, so that you may have a sense of some of the terms that will be used.

Advocacy: The act or practice of taking action by and for ourselves (or on behalf of some group or individual) upon a more powerful public or private institution, individual, or group; to gain or maintain resources or rights that will allow for the meeting of some legitimate need which has been denied or threatened.

Action Targets: Those issues and/or people which are identified as a focus for planning and action for the evaluation of community problems.

Burnout: A condition where a person ceases to do the quality of work of which she is capable. It can be caused by simple overwork, by under-support, or by over-expectation by oneself or those around us.

Caucus: A private meeting of the people involved in a change event – a demonstration or negotiation for example – for the purpose of discussing immediate strategy and/or clarifying roles within the group.

Charisma: A natural ability to inspire people.

Cinch Victory: The achieving of a particular objective that is easily achieved or won for the purpose of building credibility of the community organization and the confidence of your people. A cinch victory is usually sought at the beginning of an organization's life.

Glossary of Terms

Civil Disobedience: Actions that are outside the law, aimed at drawing to attention unequal or unjust treatment of a particular group or person. Indeed, the action may be aimed directly at a specific regulation or law (for example, lunch counter sit-ins during the civil rights protests; or the occupation of disputed lands by First Nations People; or the blocking of logging roads by environmental activists).

Coalition: The situation in which organizations agree to act in concert on particular issues of common interest, but maintain a clear identity. They give up the right to act independently on this particular issue.

Community at large: The majority of people in the society in which the target community (see below) occupies a part.

Conflict Situation: (see contest situation)

Conflict Strategy: (see contest strategy)

Consensus: A style of decision making in which all actors in a situation have the opportunity to express their ideas and feelings and to be heard seriously. It is not the same as unanimous consent. Rather it is a process which facilitates general support of whatever decision is made within a group while at the same time maintaining mutual respect among members.

Contest Situation: One in which an issue cannot be settled without confrontation between the parties; the two are too far apart on how they see their own interests. Similar to conflict situation.

Contest Strategy: One that aims at neutralizing or defeating the intentions of a person, group, or institution. Used when co-operative strategies are impossible. It should not be confused with violence. Similar to conflict strategy.

Co-optation: The use of a person's (or group's) energy and participation by government or industry to maintain the status quo and thus preserve political and social control by elites.

Culture: The sum of values, beliefs, and sets of norms, that guides our ways of relating, and of acting in the world. It provides both a glue that binds us together, and a boundary that identifies our differences from others.

Elites: A privileged minority group who have more power than the majority and who use it, sometimes obviously, sometimes covertly, to maintain their advantaged position.

Emotional tenor: The dominant feeling or feelings within a community. In effect, how a group of people feel about themselves as a group, their problems and their prospects.

Facilitation: Assisting a group or individual with a process. It is not the same as doing something for someone, but means helping them with resources (personal or instrumental) in a way that allows them to do what needs to be done.

Force Field Analysis: A popular education technique which allows us to identify and evaluate the forces - personal, organizational, historical, etc. - that are at play in a particular situation. This technique assists in developing strategy and tactics in complex situations. (See Lee and Balkwill, 1996)

Generic: A general approach that would integrate or include activities that can be seen as separate and discreet.

Goal: A desired state or result about which we are taking action expressed in general terms. (see objective)

Government: The set of institutions, elected or appointed, which provides leadership and administration for the relationships and processes that we have identified as important for our well-being.

Guerilla Theatre: A sometimes formal, sometimes informal theatrical event put on in conjunction with a demonstration to dramatize some aspect of concern to the community organization. It can range from something as stylized as a "burning in effigy" or a play to something as direct as a sit-in or the blocking of a street. Sometimes called popular theatre. (See Popular)

Hegemony: The belief system of our culture fostered by the various major institutions of society, like the media and education. For example, part of the western hegemony would be the unchallenged assumptions that capitalism and democracy are inseparable concepts, as are socialism and dictatorship.

Ideology: The way the world is understood to operate. Often our ideology is implicit and unstated (and usually culturally framed), though it is impossible to be without one.

Left Wing: Person or group that views the world in structural terms; i.e., problems like poverty and violence are seen as aspects of the structure of society which can and must be changed. Tends to value collective over individual activity.

Marshals: People chosen for supervising the actions of participants at public demonstrations like parades or rallies.

Mass-based Organization: A number of organizations form a single organization and surrender most of their individual group identity, in order to mount a powerful united front to address a range of common concerns. (Saul Alinsky was one of the most well known and an expert of this form of community organization).

Militant: Strongly determined. Again, not to be confused with violence as is sometimes the case in the media.

Networking: The development of a communication system among a group of individuals that enables them to share information.

Neo-conservative: An ideology that tries to explain the world in terms of individual desire and initiative. It is a kind of Social Darwinism (the survival of the fittest), that denies the importance of social relationships, and suggests that the best world will be built by individuals pursuing their own interests. Proponents generally resist any form of government regulation of the economy, no matter what kind of damage may result. Some of its more famous proponents are: former US president Ronald Reagan; economist Milton Friedman; and writer Ayn Rand.

Objective: A desired state or result about which we are taking action expressed in specific, concrete and measurable terms. (see goal)

Polarization: The clarifying of a situation so that the most basic positions of those involved become manifest. This then allows those involved to evaluate each others' actions in the most realistic light.

Politics: Refers to the process of allocation or redistribution of resources within a society or group. This suggests the necessity for, and use of, power.

Popular: This term is used as a qualifier throughout the book such as "popular education" and "popular action". It suggests that the people are at the centre of what is going on. It may be posed against "elite" or "expert" education or action.

Pragmatic: A concern that emphasises practical values and concerns of cause and effect; a kind of nuts and bolts approach to issues and problems.

Problem definition: The way in which the difficulties facing a community are perceived and explained. For example, a high incidence of delinquency in a geographic area can be defined in terms of psychopathology of the individuals, or structural problems (like underemployment), or something in between. Problem definition is crucial because we usually develop our strategy based on how we see the problem.

Protocol: A fairly detailed description of the way something can be completed. It might include the steps of a particular process (e.g., a survey or a demonstration).

Glossary of Terms

Radical: A person or process that aims at understanding and acting on the roots of problems; process of looking past the symptoms by analysing them.

Realistic Ideal: The best possible situation or deal that a community desires as the objective of its change efforts.

Right Wing: Person or movement who sees the status quo, particularly the issue of equality as primarily a problem of weak or bad people. Thus, there is no point (it may be dangerous) in governments' or community groups' attempting to change things. Tends to value individual over collective action. (See Neo-conservative)

Root Cause Analysis: A popular education technique that facilitates the development of thinking about the problems a community is facing and how these issues fit together. (See Lee and Balkwill, 1996)

(The) State: The network of political institutions, laws and regulations that define public social relationships; and which, in part, provide us with our identity as a civic collective.

Sociogram: A diagram representing the connections among members of a particular group. It might include such concerns as strongly positive and/or negative relationships among members. (See Lee and Balkwill, 1996)

SECTION I

Conceptualizing Community Organizing Practice

Chapter

1

SOCIAL STRUCTURAL CONTEXT OF COMMUNITY ORGANIZING PRACTICE

The exercise of power is never neutral.
—Jeremy Rifkin (1998)

Community development, as we have seen from the causes described in the introduction, is not a neutral intervention: community workers take sides (Lotz, 1995). There are a number of reasons for this. The most significant one is the unequal distribution of power in society. In this chapter we will look at how that distribution is arrived at, and consider the implications for people's everyday lives.

We live in a society, a world in fact, based on class, gender, race, and other differences. This is to say that, in our world, groups of people are defined and separated by the social, economic and occupational strata in which they find themselves (Bishop, 1994; Forcese, 1975). Given this state of affairs, we find that:

•   Power is unequally distributed: certain few individuals and groups have a great deal of influence over resources and decisions; larger numbers of individuals and groups have considerably less influence; and a smaller, though significant, number of people have virtually no influence at all.

- Because of the unequal distribution of power, opportunities to gain access to the benefits of this world are unequally apportioned.

These two facts combine to marginalize particular social, economic, or occupational levels. This results in some having (or at least having access to) many benefits, while others are left with significant deficits or burdens. Freire (1970: 44) suggests that the very fact of having "more" leads people to define having more for themselves as the ultimate "good", even at the cost of the oppressed having nothing. "For them, to be is to have and to be the class of the haves". Thus, having and not having are related aspects of reality, part of a complex socio-psychological-political-economic dynamic. Having, or being advantaged, requires that others not have and be disadvantaged.

Is there really anything so drastically wrong with inequality in society? Has not competition and the market brought us the marvels of western civilization? These are particularly pertinent questions given the present neo-conservative assault on the notion of a caring and egalitarian society that had been building in the western world since the 1940's. As long as there are relatively few abuses of power and our society builds "safety nets" for those people who "lose out", aren't things pretty humane and as they should be? After all, compared to the nineteenth century, modern Western society in general has achieved an enviable reputation for high standards of both living and individual freedom.

There are two answers to the question of inequality in contemporary Western society. First, Western societies, while better off than most countries in Eastern Europe and years ahead of so called "developing nations", are by no means utopian societies. An article in The New Yorker, hardly a bastion of radical dissent, had this comment on U.S. society:

> We have a class system in which the gap between rich and poor is widening...a permanent underclass who can find no way out of poverty. Racism continues to blight our country. Homeless people are a common sight on our city streets. (1989: 25)

The fact is, we do not live in anything like an egalitarian situation[1]. As Figure 1-1: "Distribution of Household Income" illustrates, in the industrialized nations the income of the wealthiest twenty percent of the population is roughly four-and-one-half to eight-and-one-half times that going to the poorest twenty percent. To put it in starker terms, in the United States the richest one percent of the population takes twenty-five percent of the nation's income. In Canada, the top one percent manages to accumulate twenty-two percent. Evidence that the rich are getting even richer (at least in the U.S.A.) is shown in the following:

Percentage Share of Income taken by wealthiest and poorest groups in each country		
	Poorest 20%	Wealthiest 20%
Australia (1985)	4.4	44.3
Brazil (1989)	2.1	67.5
Canada (1987)	5.7	40.2
China (1995)	5.5	47.5
France (1989)	5.6	41.9
Germany (1988)	7.0	40.3
India (1992)	8.5	42.6
Italy (1986)	6.8	41.0
Jamaica (1991)	5.8	47.5
Japan (1979)	8.7	37.5
Netherlands (1986)	8.2	36.9
Nicaragua (1993)	4.2	55.2
Nigeria (1993)	4.0	49.3
Spain (1988)	8.3	36.6
South Africa (1993)	3.3	66.3
Sweden (1981)	8.0	36.9
Uganda (1993)	6.8	48.1
United Kingdom (1988)	4.6	44.3
United States (1985)	4.7	41.9

Distribution of household income is one of the easiest measures of inequity
World Development Report 1997 (World Bank)

Figure 1.1 Distribution of Household Income

The median annual salary of all Americans in 1979 was $25,896.00, but this had shrunk to $24,700.00 in 1995 — a 4.6% decline. In contrast the top third increased by 7.9% over the same period. Incomes of the richest 5% grew to $177,518.00 in 1993, from $137,482.00 in 1973 — a 29.1% increase. The top 1% skyrocketed from $323,942.00 to $576,553.00 — a 78% rise. In the past 2 decades approximately $275 billion has been transferred from the middle class to the rich. (Cassidy 1995, in Suzuki 1995)

Benefits and deficits are not randomly distributed — the interests of some groups are achieved more or less consistently at the expense of other, usually unorganized groups. Under the U.S. social security system, for example, huge amounts of money are siphoned off to middle - and upper-income Americans (Howe & Longman, 1992). In her recent work Linda McQuaig (1998) points out how the elites of the world use unemployment, and the fear of unemployment, to put pressure on workers to "moderate" expectations regarding wages and benefits. This helps the rich in an additional way — by keeping inflation down, which allows them to make huge profits from their investments. This is a clear indication of how the rich and working people have quite divergent material interests under capitalism. This is also a clear indication of how the rich fear equality, and why working people need it.

Some of the groups particularly disadvantaged by this system are:
- women, especially those heading single parent families;[2]
- senior citizens, particularly women;
- immigrants, particularly those from the (so called) Third World;
- First Nations People;[3]
- people with physical, emotional, or mental challenges.[4]

A second issue is that inequality involves more than the simple fact of having or not having money. Disadvantaged people have less power or ability to influence their lives than the rich or middle classes. In Chapter 2 we will discuss the nature and sources of power, but for now, let us examine the social and psychological effects of being disadvantaged.

The Structure Of Empowerment and Disempowerment[5]

Empowerment, in its most practical sense, means that we feel we have an ability to influence (not totally control) our environment so that we can have our needs met. This feeling, or what White (1959) calls a sense of efficacy, is mediated by three factors or elements (see Figure 1-2):

- Instrumental - those dealing with concrete issues and needs, such as levels of employment; or access to nutrition, or to social, educational, or health services.
- Personal - those relating to our emotional and relational life, such as ability to communicate or to be mobile; or to have access to friendship or support networks. These factors may concern level of ability to communicate or understand, or the access we have for communication and understanding.
- Structural - those concerning the social, political, or economic institutions and their support or constraint for lives. Issues such as racism, sexism, or ableism would be found here.

Of course, these factors do not operate independently. Our sense of efficacy is comprised of the complex interplay of our personal abilities and the quality of the environment - instrumental and structural - in which we live.

Consider the following:

- An urban centre has a high crime rate, people without housing and a high use of social services. Police, social workers, teachers, and public health officials all point to the apathy, resistance to outside help, and destructive behaviour of the people.
- A Northern Canadian community is known for its high rate of alcohol abuse, school drop outs, adolescent suicides, unemployment, and cyclical violence. Officials, teachers, social and health services workers talk about the negative attitudes of the people as well as the magnitude of the problems.
- Statistics on mental hospital admissions show that women have a far greater likelihood of being admitted to institutions than men. Poor people are also more likely to be admitted than those in the middle class. Statistics on prison populations in Canada show that Aboriginal people are vastly over-represented. In the U.S., Blacks also are over-represented.

What are we to make of all this? That women, Native people, Black people and the poor are stupid, self-destructive, weak or evil by their nature? This social Darwinist perspective[6] has been taken by a significant number of people, even by entire societies. Europeans immigrating to North America, Australia and New Zealand based many of their genocidal actions against indigenous populations on the assertion of racial superiority. Nazis murdered 6,000,000 Jews on the basis that they were non-Aryans, inferior and harmful to the economy.

There are more humane views of social problems of course. A second theory used to explain these phenomena is the humanist liberal approach often put forward in social work. People like Germain and Gitterman (1980), for example, suggests that the fit between systems and individuals is sometimes problematic. Whitmore and Kerans (1988) note that:

after generations of being excluded, people cannot simply be suddenly invited to become involved in decisions. The result of such exclusion will not be so much unwise decisions, but a profound reluctance to enter into any decision-making process. (P.53)

Weaker members will not be able to cope and will become casualties who — rather than being punished as Social Darwinists propose — must be cared for, cured or protected. The emphasis in this approach is on the individual (Carniol, 1997).

A third approach is structural and is supported by writers such as Mulally (1997), Carniol (1997), Ruban (1976), Sennett and Cobb (1972), and Fromm (1955). It suggests that conditions of poverty or racial or gender discrimination are structured in the society and are, by their very nature, destructive to human development. The economic system, and the acquisitive social relationships produced by capitalism and bureaucracy, are largely responsible for inequality and social injustices. As Swift and Tomlinson (1991) notes:

...social, economic, cultural, and political needs arise in response to unjust structure of society; and therefore, development must ultimately contribute to the restructuring of social, economic, and political relationships....The issue of control over the development process, of how needs and solutions are articulated — at the local and national levels — becomes critical to a development model.

These are the key understandings regarding the nature, and underlying causes, of social problems. It is important to be clear that the position taken in this book is that of structural community organization. It uses an analysis of systems and relationships. What distinguishes structural work from other approaches is that we believe that all our activity needs to be grounded in the broad structural issues of class, race and gender. Further, it sees the need to root its work in perhaps less obvious, but equally important structural issues such as ability and sexual orientation, which define (most often in oppressive or discriminatory terms) the relationships of particular populations to the dominant society. This theory is particularly useful to community organizers since it is based on the notion that a crucial aspect of "what it is to be a human being" is the need to be able to act, and exert influence, on one's environment. (Biklen, 1983; Freire, 1970)

Environment And Efficacy

Robert W. White (1959) theorizes that an important basis for individual growth is the development of an understanding that we are different from our environment. This is accomplished by experiencing the consequences of our actions. He also suggests that the development of one's ego is based on "a growing sense of competence". White says that our ability to feel competent, and thus behave in a competent manner, rests with our ability to actually experience competence. The environment then, as well as the individual's own talents, has an important impact on one's aptitude to feel and be successful. It must be amenable to our activity.

Another psychologist, Norman Maier (1961), found that when he put animals in situations where their behaviour could not create "consequences" in their environment; and where they were prevented from learning how to make their actions count, they developed behaviours that apparently ignored the environment and its responses. Behaviour often became self-destructive. Maier termed this "frustration instigated behaviour" because it was focussed on dealing with frustration, not on achieving a positive goal.

Later, Maier and Ellen applied the theory to human conditions. They suggested that if a situation is severe enough, and of sufficient duration, a "frustration threshold" will be crossed and the inner tension of the person will become the dominant cause of behaviour:

> *Such behaviour is determined largely by conditions inside the organism, so that the expression of emotions and feelings, rather than what they achieve, characteristically accompany behaviour selected under conditions of frustration. (Maier and Ellen, 1965: 100).*

In other words, a sufficiently frustrated person will act, not to deal with actual objective conditions – which may not be amenable to action anyway – but with the anxiety associated with the frustrated condition. He will tend to act on whatever, or whoever, is handy.

Richard Ball (1973) became interested in frustration instigated behaviour and applied it to a community situation - areas where social dysfunction was reported to be high and of long duration, some of the groups of southern Appalachia in the United States. He suggested that Maier's notions fitted these situations – the people had a long history of "unremitting physical, economical and social frustration, repeatedly blocked, pressured and defeated by their environment". He suggested that "self-destructive" attitudes of fatalism and apathy, or behaviour of intra-familial and community violence, for example, were actually frustration responses. "Such behaviour may be difficult for the motivation-oriented observer to comprehend, but it is quite likely to provide relief from the tensions of extreme and prolonged frustration." He explained that people deprived of the ability to act effectively on their environment will become increasingly anxious over time. In situations of prolonged anxiety, they will resort to any behaviours that will provide even temporary soothing of the internal discomfort.

This is an important analysis with which to view the communities stuck with little or no resources to influence their lives or their environments. As human beings we strive to render ourselves and our environment **understandable, predictable and manageable**. To the extent that we are successful in meeting material, social and spiritual needs, we experience feelings of competence and a sense of well-being that White (1959) refers to as efficacy. When we are unsuccessful — when things get out of our control — we experience feelings of incompetence, or non-efficacy, and lack a sense of well-being. If we think in terms of the empirical work of Maier and its application by Ball, we would refer to feelings of anxiety.

There is a dynamic relationship among these three important variables. Our self-image influences our behaviour within our environments.

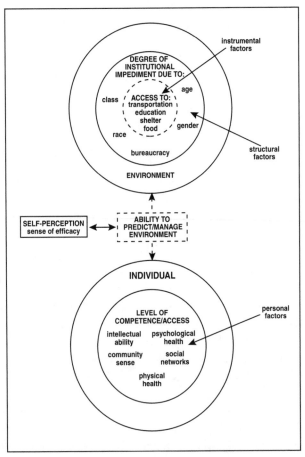

Figure 1-2   The Structuring of Self-efficacy

This relationship is illustrated in Figure 1-2: The Structuring of Self-efficacy. Likewise, our personal abilities, such as intelligence, are developed by our relationship with our environment which has an instrumental dimension (the actual access to the necessities of life) and a structural dimension (the degree of classism which will have an effect on our ability to access necessities).

Thus, there is a dynamic relationship between our personal abilities and the environment in which they are activated or blocked. This dynamic has an effect on how we perceive ourselves; and that perception (of our ability to manage our environment) in turn affects how we try to deal with our environment. The positive side of this relationship is presented in Figure 1-3.[8]

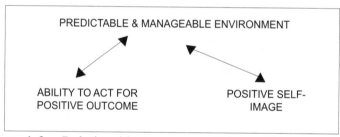

PREDICTABLE & MANAGEABLE ENVIRONMENT

ABILITY TO ACT FOR POSITIVE OUTCOME

POSITIVE SELF-IMAGE

Figure 1-3   Relationship between positive self-image and the connection between a predictable and manageable environment and one's ability to act for a positive outcome.

If we live in an environment that is predictable and manageable, we will be generally able to act within it to satisfy our needs. (This, of course, does not preclude struggle). Further, we will be able to perceive and experience our success. This will lead us to feel good about who we are and about our environment, which we see as a relatively benign place. Our positive image of the environment encourages us to act in and with it, perhaps rendering it even more manageable and reinforcing the notion of ourselves as creative, productive individuals. The type of behaviour that is likely to emerge from this dynamic will, we suggest, be purposive and humane; that is, it will be shaped to attain the best results for ourselves and our environment in both the short and long term. As researcher Ellen Langer states:

When people feel they can exercise some control over their environment, they seek out new information, plan, strategize, and so on – they behave mindfully and, as they engage in control behaviour, it is this mindful enactment of perceived control behaviour, that yields the positive psychological and physical consequences described.... (1983: 207-8)

What will occur, however, if this dynamic relationship possesses negative connections? What if the environment is unpredictable, and/or unmanageable? What if our actions are unable to produce positive results for ourselves? Figure 1-4 suggests the result of this relationship.

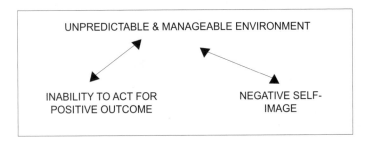

Figure 1-4   Relationship between negative self-image and the connection between an unpredictable and unmanageable environment and one's inability to act for a positive outcome.

Simply put, if we live in an environment that is socially and materially unpredictable, and unmanageable, our activity within it will not be need-fulfilling. As we experience our lack of ability we begin to feel badly both about ourselves as people and our environment, perceiving it with dread or apprehension, as a malignant or dangerous place.[8] We begin to feel disempowered or anxious. Our negative image of the environment and our anxiety will discourage us from acting in any planned or coherent fashion. Our environment likely becomes less manageable and our image of ourselves is one of passivity, powerlessness, and victimization. We become preoccupied, not with creation, but with survival - or simply with the relieving of anxiety

(Ball, 1973: 74). Langer (1983: 207), reporting on research with individuals who experience a chronic loss of control, states:

> *Here we consider situations in which people over time gradually and insidiously lose control. When people feel a chronic loss of control they don't take risks and they retreat into an all too familiar world.*

The type of behaviour that is likely to emerge from this dynamic will lack an overall sense of purpose and will be entered on immediate need-satisfaction, which may involve the avoidance of internal pain or frustration. It will be shaped to attain quick, anxiety-reducing results, relative only to the individual and his or her immediate feelings of anxiety. This response neglects long term needs as well as the needs of other human beings and of the environment.[9]

A passage from Sennett & Cobb (1973: 22) eloquently presents the feeling of what it is like to be rendered marginal or ineffectual within one's environment:

> *... images in his conversation concerning the poor [including his father], both white and black, ...fuse material deprivation with chaotic, arbitrary and unpredictable behaviour: he sees poverty...as depriving men of the capacity to act rationally, to exercise self-control ... [D]ignity means, specifically, moving toward a position in which he deals with the world in some controlled, emotionally restrained way.*

A word of caution is necessary here. We do not propose that the environment must be totally hostile to our actions for it to affect our self-image and our ability to act constructively. We refer to situations where we experience that our actions are irrelevant to a desired outcome: a situation where we can be sure of doing neither good nor ill. Such an environment might have benign aspects; for example, some nice people (teachers, social workers, politicians) might be doing some nice things for us, but it is not within our power to influence them to our advantage, or to anyone else's. As Fromm (1964: 63) notes, even things can be treated nicely. *They* do things to, or for, us. Our activity counts for nothing, and we have no power. Fromm (1964: 57) states further:

> ... *"freedom from" political shackles is not a sufficient condition. If love for life is to develop, there must be freedom "to": freedom to create and to construct, to wonder and to venture. Such freedom requires that the individual be active and responsible, not a slave or a well fed cog in the machine.*

What else is mental health but man's capacity to act according to his true interest?

When considering the nature of community development, then, the following things seem to be true:

- Disadvantaged people will have to organize - to develop and rescue themselves - because it is unlikely that they are going to be rescued en masse by those with the resources (Carniol 1997, Freire, 1970; Piven and Cloward, 1977). **Relevant energy for change** is only going to come from within disadvantaged communities as they use the awareness of themselves and their situation (Adamson et al. 1987; Bishop 1994; Freire, 1970); and the power of their belief; and their numbers in collective action (Bloomberger 1969; Antone et al. 1986). Numbers and conviction are often the only initial power resource the disadvantaged have but, as stated earlier, numbers are only potent if they are organized and cohesive (Alinsky, 1971). As Booth (1974) points out, numbers of organized people are the foundation and means of deliberate social change. Theorists may argue about why and how people act together (to alter the relationships of power in their society) as do Piven and Cloward (1977), but all would agree that large numbers of people are essential for a change process.

- Another apparent aspect of community organization is its "therapeutic" quality. People who are organized and who become effective in rendering their environment relatively more malleable are more likely to perceive themselves differently, as subjects not objects, as people who develop a vision of a better world (a more long range purposeful act) and who can act coherently to achieve it. The organizing endeavour can be seen as the process of bringing people together to share their experiences, create a vision, and develop means to act to attain that vision.

Example: Members of the Chetwynd Project, in Toronto, beautifully articulated the healing potential of community development. They suggested that understanding and sharing their experiences as single parents, immigrants, or visible minorities had reduced their sense of isolation. Becoming involved in action to improve their situation reduced their sense of isolation, and of themselves as victims. They started to see their abilities and how they might use them in other areas of their lives.

Some Practical Concepts

Community
A community is a **group of people**. As such, it is subject to the various laws that have been discovered or constructed by social scientists to deal with how we organize our relationships. The laws may not always agree because (as Warren (1983) points out) there is a variety of ways for understanding the notion of community. Though we can think about community in many ways, we are first going to focus on a way here that allows us to understand the importance of community and community organizing.

Community as Interface
This perspective focuses on the degree of complexity or sophistication that exists within the organization of relationships at various levels of society. For example, at the personal level we are individuals — complex beings, generally living in some sort of set of friendship and/ or family relationships. The institutional level of organization, which includes the state and the economy, represents a more distant and

complex array of relationships. They are organized much more formally and impersonally, with relationships generally being contractual and legal. Figure 1-5: "Levels of Societal Relationships" illustrates that the lives we live "in community" represent a middle ground or interface between the personal areas of life - individual and family life as well as friendship networks - and the institutional level - the state and economic

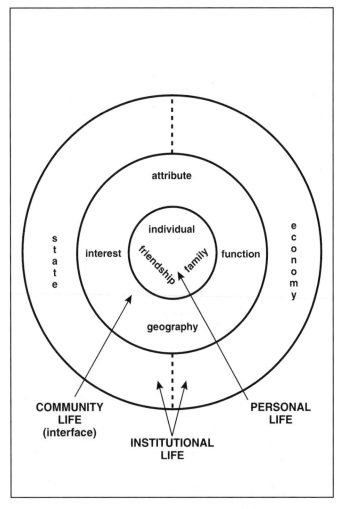

Figure 1-5: Levels of Societal Relationships

organizations and activity. One definition of community (Ponting 1986, p.155) sees it as a network (or potential network) of reciprocal interpersonal and inter-organizational relations - made up of one or more groups of individuals, families and organizations - and wherein there exists (or potentially exists) a shared sense of belonging. From this very general conception we can begin to see that community is an important focus for attention and organizing. It is neither as personal as family life, nor as impersonal or formal as institutional life, but partaking of both. It mediates the needs and demands of the personal on institutional life, and visa versa.

In practical terms there are essentially three types of communities. There can be some overlap, but it is useful to think in the following terms:

Geographic People living in the same physical area – such as an urban neighbourhood or a rural village.

Function or Attribute People who share or possess a common and essential factor - perhaps gender, race, religion, or socioeconomic status. Unions are found in this group – all workers for a department store chain or auto workers, for example.

Interest This is really a sub-type of community of "function". A strong common interest can be an essential defining characteristic of a group – people who band together to fight the construction of an expressway, to seek funding for some charity or special event, or to fight a polluting industry.

To be a community, the group will also have distinct **boundaries**. The geographical area it occupies or the attributes members share will be distinct from other groups. It must be recognized, or have the potential to be recognized, as having an identity of its own. For example, a group of people working within an industry may not appear to be distinct as a group. However, once they begin to unionize they become clearly visible as a specific entity.

A community will have some **consciousness of itself**, its boundaries and/or focus (Roberts, 1979 :45). It may only be a potential consciousness, but members must ultimately recognize themselves as a distinct entity. A number of babies, three to ten months old would not be considered a community; but a group of Aboriginal people could.

The fact of membership in a community may provide each member with particular **benefits or deficits**. For example, a single parent receiving assistance under a government social welfare program, (a member of a community of attribute) can be seen as having the benefit (such as it is) of public financial support. At the same time, we know that this support was less than adequate to maintain them above the poverty line. In the fall of 1995, the Ontario Government cut the already meagre allotment by 21.6%. Obviously, a person in this situation possesses an attribute that is beneficial and "deficital" at the same time.

Community as a Political Entity

We need a politics that speaks more directly to the heart, and to the repressed need for social connectedness that lies there bruised and stunted.

—Barbara Ehrenreich (1993)

Keeping in mind that a community occupies the mediating circle between personal and institutional life, it follows that it is a **political entity**. It has a self-interest, or set of interests, that correlates with some parts of its environment, and runs counter to others. For example, a housing co-operative – a community of attribute and geography – may have interests that correlate quite well with the municipality in which it exists. Good sewers, transportation and education are examples of areas on which everyone would agree. However, if the municipality were to allow a polluting industry to be built next to it – for tax and employment advantages – the members could find their interests very much at odds with other segments of the municipality. Thus, over time a community's political nature will be quiet and unseen at times; and, by the necessity of its self-interest, be high profile at others. Again, power is an important dimension (see below).

The political nature of community, and thus community work, has been particularly accentuated in the last decade. The advent of four dynamics - diversity; globalization and technological innovation; the attack of the right, or corporate interests, on the disadvantaged and working / middle class; and, finally, the strategy of selling the inevitability of these changes - has had profound effects on community, whether geographically or functionally defined[10].

1. Diversity - within and among communities

While a community has never been a single entity - there have always been subgroupings of family, or interest, or class, etc. - communities in North America have become more diverse. Poverty, conflict, and oppression in many parts of the world; and recruitment from areas such as Asia, has brought a great number of diverse groups to North America. This has resulted in "racial and cultural diversity" becoming an increasingly important dynamic in community life. A second aspect is, the increased number of marginalized groups (gays, lesbians, and psychiatric survivors, for example) that have found their voices, and wish to enter the mainstream of community life. Diversity has added complexity and stress to community life and work (Lee et el., 1996). Some even believe that it is dangerous and should be played down (Rubin and Rubin, 1986). What this would probably accomplish, however, is the subjugation of important and legitimate "voices" - which would simply reproduce unjust power relations, and cause resentment. Of course we cannot, and never will, work with the "whole" community. No community worker rounds up all the members of a particular community and starts to "develop" them. We work with segments of a community, the leadership, emerging leaders, work groups and interest groups. Our effort is with the people who are going to do the real work of mobilizing all the people they can in order to undertake the necessary change strategies. At the same time - while we look for leadership, interests, and issues - we must seek to understand the diversities that lie, sometime hidden, within the community. We need to learn to deal across difference - to use the energy of diversity in positive ways (Narayan, 1994;. Erlich and Rivera, 1995).

2. *Globalization and Technological Innovation.*

As Rifkin (1995) notes, technology - particularly information technology and the much freer flow of capital - has allowed many corporations to cut ties to local communities, and seek around the world for cheap labour and lower taxation. This has undercut the material base of North American communities. This is decreasing the number of well paid wage earners and tax payers, which makes it more difficult for communities to "care" for their members. A powerful picture of what the globalized economy is about, is presented by Atkinson and Elliot (1998):

> *This is the 'New Command Economy', in which capital is free and working people have been nationalized. Unemployment is a fact of life; huge inequalities have opened up in income and in wealth, the private sector does what it likes and the public sector does what it is told. The very instability left by the rampaging wolf of global capital makes necessary much more stringent social controls; as jobs move out of the inner-city neighbourhood so the closed circuit cameras and 'zero-tolerance' police move in. And the new culture of control is a make-work scheme for politicians and administrators; having abandoned any pretense at managing the economy, they channel their energies into managing the citizenry.*

It adds a further element for consideration as we try to help people identify issues, and mobilize for action. The energy levels may be quite low in the face of real and severe crisis. As one community worker expressed: "People are feeling such desperation they want something, anything, that will answer some immediate needs. They don't feel they can wait. They often don't seem to have the energy and patience for organizing." This is a dynamic that will have to be clearly understood by community workers, not so we will simply give up, but so we can work with people to help them develop energy and hope.

3. Attack of the Right

This attack has three parts. The first is the assault on the idea of the welfare state which, whatever its faults, means so much to those injured by industrial capitalism. The second is devolution of responsibility for services to the community. This is a delicate issue. Many, such as McKnight (1995) have argued that the community is the best place for dealing with local problems. The difficulty is that most of the devolution requires funding which only the state, through taxing authority, can provide. While companies and their money flee our communities (or threaten to unless given sweetheart tax deals and low labour costs), right wing think tanks and corporate elites have mounted fairly successful attacks on important elements of the welfare state - like progressive taxation; and the provision of public health, education and social services. The effects are terrible. Omatsu (1993) talking about the U.S.A. puts it this way:

The corporate offensive...brutally destroyed grassroots groups in the African American community. This war against the poor ripped apart the social fabric of neighbourhoods across America leaving them vulnerable to drugs and gang violence. The inner cities became the home of the 'underclass', and a new politics of inner-directed violence and despair.

A third part of the assault has been an increasing appeal to devolve "responsibility" to the community. A nostalgic notion has been sold that communities used to completely care for their members without the intervention of the state (McKnight, 1995). The fact of course is that while there is some truth here (there has been a decrease in families caring for elderly parents, for example), such a notion ignores the fact that historically the bulk of the caring was left to women, and that communities (particularly poor ones) experienced extreme variations in the levels and quality of services. It also ignores the involvement of women in the paid workforce. As we have said, the communities we deal with today are not the homogeneous, place-based groups of the 1920's or 1950's. They have different strengths, different stressors, and presently are under attack from the very governments and right wing interests that so hypocritically extol their merits. It is part of the community worker's assignment to be aware of this; and to assist community members to reflect on it so that realistic objectives can be identified, and people can recognize the importance of joining with other communities to work for appropriate community supports.

4. The Myth of Inevitability

One of the most insidious parts of the strategy of assault has been the selling of the notion that the trend to global markets (the domination of technological innovations and downloading of services) is somehow part of the forces of history - a kind of social evolutionary process. This is an ideology that obscures the fact that all these decisions are being made by human beings with particular interests in advancing these trends (Saul, 1995). We are urged to believe that the "market" dictates that corporations move to areas where wages are low, and worker protections and civil rights are poor or nonexistent. This story obscures the fact that markets are human inventions; and liberates the corporate high roller - the government and the disadvantaged - from thinking that any of us can, or should, do anything (McQuaig, 1998). The idea that we are agents (citizens) who can act, is crucial to the health of a community. Remember Langer (1983: 207): "When people feel a chronic loss of control they don't take risks; and they retreat into an all too familiar world." If the idea that we can act is successfully undercut, much of the energy for progressive social change will disappear. As community workers, we must assist people to resist the idea that they cannot act, and to search for the power to assert influence in their lives.

Power

Power is defined here as **the degree to which we are able to act to influence our environment** - to get things done, or make things happen; or to keep things from getting done, or happening. Power is essential in bringing about positive change.

There are five elements of power: money, information, numbers, status, and belief or conviction.

1. Money

Money is an obvious one. We see it clearly in the ability of rich multi-national corporations to influence or control their environment. Speeter (1978: 52) makes the point that "corporations can afford to lobby, influence the public through the media, and buy their way out of certain predicaments. The larger the corporation and its resources, the more resistant it is to attack or reform". For example, columnist Dalton Camp (1998: F3) points to how powerful tobacco companies (by using the power of their political campaign contributions to dictate the way the elected representatives would vote) subverted the attempts of U.S. legislators to "address the problems of kids getting hooked on tobacco.":

*The American tobacco companies have once again cashed
promissory notes and resumed their dominance of the Republican party and its representatives in the United States Senate.
The bipartisan bill aimed at the problem of kids'getting hooked
on tobacco...has been sandbagged by the ...usual coalition of
tobacco pushers and free marketeers....Pray observe this salu-
tary illustration of Big Tobacco vs. the little man....The tobacco
interests have spent 40 to 50 million (someone said 100 million) on television, trying to provide cover for the Republican
effort to stop the bill's passage.*

This power is in contrast with the ability of the poor to affect their
environment. Bregha (1971:76) states that the inability of the lower
middle-class "to secure proper housing, higher education, and better-
paying jobs is forcing it out of the so called mainstream of Canadian
life." As well, the poor have had little impact on our political system –
they tend not to vote and, as Adams points out, rarely complain en
masse (1970). Some argue that political science lectures on "the theory
of representative democracy" (the familiar tale about how we elect the
people who govern us) sorely needs updating. There is the question of
who funds the parties, and what effect it has on the policies they pursue.
For instance, in Canada in 1993, the Liberals received about $100,000
from each of the five major banks, and another $100,000 or so from
each of the five securities firms under bank control (Cameron 1994,
p.4). We should not be surprized to find that government listens to the
rich more than to working class people.

2. Information

Information comes in many forms – technical, academic, "privileged"
(from within an elite system) – and is a central source of power.
Information issues occupy a central place in the public's attention, and
are high on the agenda of business and government. There is an
increased awareness of the role of information in the democratic process.
Paton (1994: 20) states, that "inclusion, participation, and open
government are empty concepts". At the level of public policy,

government has access to tremendous amounts of data that its departments develop. It is generally unavailable to ordinary citizens. Ken Rubin, Ottawa's "king of access to information", claims that the access to information legislation is in fact a secrecy act (Webster, 1997: 20).[11] Citizens tend to be in a reactive position and, in effect, have difficulty challenging that which is inaccessible to public scrutiny.

The relationship is one of power, and the power is exclusive to government and its bureaucracy. There is no room in this collectivity for the disadvantaged, the service receivers, or even the public. Most individual citizens have neither the information, nor the technical ability to digest the information that they may find. The implications are serious for all citizens, but as a Canadian social critic points out, they have particular relevance for the poor. "Ultimately, the confused multiplicity of bureaucratic systems keeps the poor on a treadmill of marginal living while simultaneously robbing them of pride and the ability to get back into society" (Adams, 1970: 67).

As we have seen, information is particularly crucial in the private sector. Large corporations possess massive concentrations of wealth, and are able to develop and exchange great amounts of data of which they become the sole proprietors. A clear example was the oil industry's estimates of reserves in the 1970s. Until 1973, reserves were estimated by the industry as secure for many, many years. When the international price of petroleum suddenly quadrupled, however, the companies changed their predictions sharply downward (Laxer and Martin, 1976). This is not an isolated case. The savings and loan scandal in the U.S. showed how information was kept from the public until the money had been totally misspent and a bailout (costing the public purse billions) had to be developed.

3. Numbers

We equate large numbers of people with power, most often as it is exercised through the vote. While this is an important and much-praised foundation of democratic society, it is only a token source of power that is used intermittently.[12] (Every four years in the U.S. presidential elections, every four or five years in parliamentary systems, every two or three years for municipal councils.) Macpherson (1977, p.77) argues that our present system of democracy can best be termed a "pluralist elitist model".

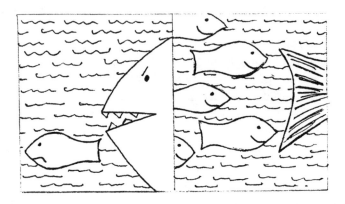

This is not to suggest that Western democratic institutions are useless. Clearly they are superior to dictatorship, but the vote does not, and cannot, represent a de facto reasonable exercise of power for the citizen (Fromm, 1955). It is important for citizens to organize to demand access to institutions which will reflect their genuine needs and perspectives; independent of powerful political parties (and their imperatives), and of civil service bureaucracies (and theirs) (Adamson et al.,1988). Issue groups (for peace and life, women's rights, Indigenous Peoples' rights), service groups (women's shelters, housing or work co-operatives, day care centres or senior citizen drop-ins), or even short-term lobby or pressure organizations (a group resisting an expressway or a specific piece of harmful legislation) are the life blood of a genuine living democracy. This type of political involvement potentially allows for people's power to result in empowerment and social justice.

4. Status

The power of **status** comes from a person's (or group's) formal or informal right to act in particular areas or on particular issues. Elected officials are the most obvious examples. We also have appointed officials who derive power from being placed in authority by elected officials. People can also gain power by acquiring some socially-recognized credentials – doctors, lawyers and university professors obtain a certain power in their particular, narrow fields. We grant tremendous authority to these people. Often this kind of power can be used against ordinary citizens. While those in authority often deserve respect, authority must ultimately be granted by the people in a way that is not self-perpetuating and oppressing.

5. Belief or Conviction[13]

> *Those who lose dreaming are lost.*
> *—Australian Aboriginal Proverb*

Deeply held belief (in a way of life or a just cause) has been a strong element of power for many community based campaigns. Fromm (1961) refers to this as a spiritual aspect of life - a sense of purpose higher than simply accepting the circumstances of our lives. Beliefs can bring people together and provide us with courage to persevere in a difficult struggle. The majority of the organizers described in the first chapter, and the people with whom they worked, were motivated by the sense of purpose that transcended the rejections and disappointments that they encountered. In an ironic way, the importance of belief in community work is underlined by the way contemporary political and economic elites have tried to suggest that human beings are simply economic animals; and that the market, plus impersonal historical forces, are the last and best arbiters of our lives. Belief in non-material values - spirituality, human brother/sisterhood, for example - are deeply threatening to a capitalist-materialistic position.

Clearly the power of belief can be misused. Fundamentalist movements (like fascism and some religious groups) have manipulated and oppressed people, and have caused great harm. Thus we must make a point of reflecting seriously on what, and how, beliefs are being used in the communities.

Organization Structure

Building a community organization that is consistent with the values of participation and democracy is important and difficult. The fall of the Berlin Wall, and the toppling of the dictatorship in Russia, have shown that good intentions, or simply changing the people at the top, are not enough to bring about social changes that will guarantee genuine equality and liberation from oppression. Piven and Cloward (1977) argue that the act of organization-building may in fact retard and frustrate real change. It is hard, however, to imagine an increase in the rights of women, or of Indigenous people (for example), without strong organizations.

Organization-building is an important aspect of furthering the cause of empowerment and social justice (Kahn, 1982; Biklen, 1983; Roberts, 1979; Alinsky, 1971; Booth, 1974). Even Piven and Cloward agree that positive social change will not come about without some structure-building (1977). They argue, however, that the vision and energy necessary to accomplish real social change gets drained off in the minutiae of system maintenance. Still, for most of human history it is difficult to find the achievement of real social change without organizations. As pointed out earlier, however, the building of strong organizations does not guarantee genuine humane social change, or any social change for that matter.

Models of organization that we have tend to come from the corporate sector (see Figure 1-6: Bureaucratic organization model). The image of the "lean and mean" bureaucratic pyramid is pervasive. People naturally tend to choose what they know, and what has been held up as successful. Important institutions, like the media, maintain this business hegemony, generally portraying capitalist business structures as efficient and effective. Institutions, such as the education system, structure relationships among people that mirror those in capitalist industry. (Bowles and Gintis, 1976) The traditional organizational model has a powerful grip in North America.

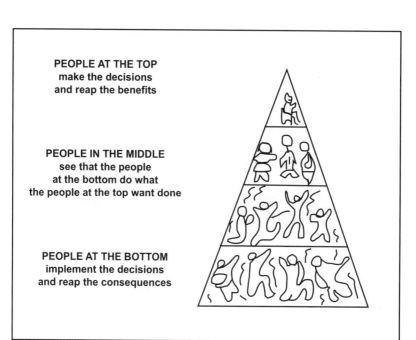

PEOPLE AT THE TOP
make the decisions
and reap the benefits

PEOPLE IN THE MIDDLE
see that the people
at the bottom do what
the people at the top want done

PEOPLE AT THE BOTTOM
implement the decisions
and reap the consequences

Figure 1-6 Bureaucratic organization model

It is not surprising that we tend to use the bureaucratic model despite the fact that it is both undemocratic and sometimes oppressive. Peoples' organizations desiring to "change the system" often develop bureaucratic structures and end up reproducing the traits of business and government structures: the exact traits that, the people have complained, have been messing up their lives for years – rigidity, unresponsiveness and nepotism (Speeter, 1978). It is important to note that progressive groups - First Nations and women, for example (Weeks, 1994; Gilroy, 1990) - and people involved in worker co-operatives are trying for alternative non-hierarchic structuring of their organizations (Lakey et al., 1995).

Funding agencies, government or private, tend to demand the development of familiar corporate structures before money is granted. To access funding, the community conforms in order to satisfy the "accountability" requirements of the funder. While this is understandable from the perspective of funders, it works against the principle of democratic accountability to the people who are the foundation of the organization.

Power is a seductive commodity. As Lord Acton said, "Power tends to corrupt".[14] As we gain power, there is a temptation to exercise it immediately rather than share it. It is difficult to take "the long view" - that the organization is the message as well as the instrument of institutional change (Speeter, 1978). Freire (1970) points out how difficult it is for deprived people not to mirror their oppressors. There is a tendency to build organizations that are oriented more to controlling member behaviour than liberating the human spirit.

Approaches To Community Organizing Practice

Traditionally there have been three ways of conceptualizing the manner in which community organization sets about its tasks. This three-way view is articulated in the classic article by Rothman and Tropman (1987) under the headings "Locality Development", "Social Action" and "Social Planning". While they make the point that these are abstract models, and that in "real life" they often overlap; they suggest that community organization is essentially practiced within one of these frameworks. (Rothman and Tropman, 1987)

"Locality Development" emphasizes broadly based participation, co-operation, voluntarism, education and community initiative to achieve community determined goals. The "Social Planning" approach focuses on professional expertise and technical know-how, that operate out of a centralized planning context, to overcome designated social problems and "guide complex change processes." A "Social Action" approach aims to organize disadvantaged populations to make demands for

MODEL	SOCIAL PLANNING	LOCALITY DEVELOPMENT	SOCIAL ACTION	PRAGMATIC
DESCRIPTION	experts using technical expertise -identify & plan how to address designated social problems	community initiative to identify & achieve community goals	organization of disadvantaged to make demands for social justice	addresses complex organizational & developmental community needs & social/political constraints
RELATIONSHIP OF WORKER & COMMUNITY	people are objects of intervention	people are subjects & co-workers on problems	people are subjects & co-workers on problems	people are subjects & co-workers on problems
PRIMARY WORKER ROLE	expert planner	catalyst/facilitator	catalyst/agitator	facilitator/agitator & strategist
PRIMARY MEANS	statistics & reports	consensus	conflict, confrontation & negotiation	conflict, confrontation & consensus
ENDS	improved services	suitable sharing of community resources among members	readjustment of power between community & institutions	empowerment and social justice

Figure 1-7: Conceptualizing the Pragmatic Approach

"increased resources or treatment more in accordance with social justice."

The focus of this book is on strategies that incorporate elements primarily of the locality development and social action models. The reasons for this will become apparent in the following sections. The approach suggested here will be referred to as a "pragmatic approach". (See Figure 1-7: Conceptualizing the Pragmatic Approach).

A Pragmatic Approach

The three models, described above, have some important commonalities. They also have some differences. (See Figure 1-7: Conceptualizing the Pragmatic Approach). Social planning, in particular, appears to be "more different" than the other two. With its emphasis on central planning and professional expertise, it defines its relationship with its target population very differently than do locality development and social action models. For the social planner, the people and/or services are the "objects" of intervention. For the community worker, the people are "subjects", co-workers on the problems. Thus a person employed as a locality development worker, or one working as an action organizer, is working with and among the people. A social planner, on the other hand, generally works with other professionals on behalf of a group. This difference is crucial because the worker's reference group will be quite different. Working day-by-day with a group of professionals who use statistics and reports gives one a different perspective on one's clientele than if the organizer is actually among them every day. Because of this, the social planner is more likely to see things from a so-called "objective" point of view, but also from the point of view of her professional colleagues. A locality development or social action worker, on the other hand, is more likely to have her professional view influenced by those of her clientele. It should be noted that there are risks and advantages to these situations of relative intimacy.

1. Risks of working in "relative intimacy"

There is a danger of losing perspective, of seeing things in a unidirectional manner and missing an important part of the picture. This can lead to a loss of creativity, an inability to see various options. After all, if intimate experience with the problem were all that was required, disadvantaged folks would have solved their own problems long ago.

Intimacy can also lead to complacency – "if I'm with the people I automatically understand them, and what they need and want." Being with people does not guarantee that we will listen to them, or understand them or their problems. (Narayan, 1994)

2. Advantages of working in "relative intimacy"

Paulo Freire (1970) has probably written the most forcefully on the importance of "relationships" with the people with whom the organizer is working. There are two essential points that he makes:

- Disadvantaged people have a particular view of their reality which must be used as a starting point for action. The organizer must be led by the people, and can only be led by them if she is with them in a very concrete way. The emphasis is placed, not on a doubtful objectivity, but on gaining an understanding of the client's perspective. A community organizer with a locality development focus, who was employed by a child welfare organization, stated:

  "The people who I took my cues from changed a lot once I came out to the community every day. After I was there a couple of months, I started to realize that I was defining problems differently than when I was working in a more traditional role out of the central office. Some of my social work colleagues charged that I was losing my objectivity. I saw it differently – that I'd exchanged the point of reference that informed my objectivity."

- Another notion crucial to understanding transformational social change is the idea that as organizers we are not "giving" people a "better life", but are assisting them to struggle and build it themselves. This notion of participation, of "building with" not "designing for", describes a profoundly different relationship with disadvantaged people than that which educators, social workers or politicians have traditionally attempted.

A close relationship with the people with whom we work allows us to be seen as human beings, and our techniques to be seen as human and fallible - not as some mystifying magic, but a set of behaviours and instruments that people can test for themselves. A crucial difference between the social planning model on the one hand, and a pragmatic locality development/social action model on the other, is that of the "immediacy" of the relationship. This immediacy might be termed solidarity – the intimate identification of one's goals and actions with those of the members of the community.

Citizens And Victims

Although the pragmatic approach represents an attempt to integrate key aspects of locality development and social action, it does not use every aspect of each model. Rather, it creates the base of a model which will be useful with a wide variety of community groups, issues and situations. When a worker is acting in the community, however, she is not practicing a particular model, but attempting to deal with real people who are trying to get themselves together to influence some aspect of their environment. This requires the development of skills and strategies that can be general in their application.

The differences between locality development and social action appear initially to be difficult to reconcile, for they involve, in at least a general way, separate ends and separate means. The end, for social action, is the readjustment of power within society, such that the community is on a significantly more equal footing with major institutions of power. In contrast, the goal of locality development is the equitable sharing of community resources among its own membership. In the former, the community member is perceived as the victim of an invidious power structure, while in the latter he is seen as a citizen and member of a collective.

Out of these differing conceptions of membership and ends emerges a differing orientation to means. Social action stresses the need to engage in conflict with the oppressor, while locality development suggests that citizens use co-operative or consensus techniques among themselves to reach mutually advantageous decisions.

These differences, on the surface, are significant. However, if we attend carefully to Rothman's statement - that in practice there is much overlap - we can examine the "reality" with which the models deal and develop a pragmatic approach that has important implications for practice.

A community is not static. It has a history. People leave or join it. It can experience periods of internal conflict, as well as a degree of unity and tranquillity. It can experience wins and losses. It has connections to its environment (Roberts, 1979). Thus, to view a community as only a group of citizens, or only as victims, is unrealistic. With groups of disadvantaged people, in particular, the structure of their lives demands that they be seen as both **citizens and victims**. People often have to deal with both the pressures of external oppression – unfair labour practices, racism, environmental pollution or sexism – and serious intra-group misunderstanding and conflict. It is not uncommon for a disadvantaged community to experience divisions of class or to have sexism or racism in its midst, as well as more personal problems of communication or personality conflict. The interplay between historical development and contemporary interaction produces a complex set of dynamics that is not amenable to intervention based on one dimensional thinking.

> **Example:** A service provider, who became involved in the Chetwynd Project in one community, stated that working with some of the women had changed her view of them as simply victims. "I know they still had difficulties with their kids, and many didn't have job skills; but they had ideas and they could get them across. Some could really organize an event. I can't

look at poor people the same way anymore."

The pragmatic approach attempts to deal with the complex organizational and developmental needs of the community. It incorporates aspects from both of Rothman and Tropman's formulations: that change must be community-directed; and, that the process of community-building is of central importance. However, the model presented here will approach the problem in a way that addresses an important dichotomy in community development: conflict versus consensus.

Equity: Consensus And Conflict

Community problems are caused principally by the unequal distribution of power in society. Concern for a more equitable sharing of resources and power, both inside and outside the group, is essential. There is a tendency to think of co-operation and conflict as being two ends of some sort of ideological continuum. In the model offered here, they are seen in more pragmatic terms. We can expect to find situations, both internal and external, that require both consensus and conflict strategies.

A problem with some organizers is that they fail to take into account that they are building both communities and organizations. Without people organized and/or structured to work on their common interests, nothing can be accomplished. Organizers must be able to see members of the community as fellow human beings who can give more than merely political support on one or two issues. Like soldiers who may have joined the army out of economic necessity or because of their political ideals, they endure and persist because of the caring for each other that they develop. We cannot argue too strongly for the building of consensus, and for the fostering of networks of support within the community.

There are two reasons for stressing the notion of locality development within social action. The first is that in striving to overcome a "social wrong", or in building a "social right", a great deal of stress will be felt by the participants, as well as by the organizer. The establishment of positive human relationships (a major aspect of a sense of community) will alleviate the negative effects of stress (Speck & Attneave: 1973). The second reason is that there will be internal conflict as various individuals and interest groups - who hold divergent views - try to have their views prevail (See Chapter 7; Dealing With Internal Opposition). Conflict cannot and should not be avoided. It can, and should, be managed. This is made possible by the development of an atmosphere of clear and direct communication; and warm respectful relationships. This does not mean that community organization should become a series of therapeutic group encounters - only that organization development is not an end on its own. An organizer must attend to the personal, political, and organizational needs of her constituency or risk failure. If community work is transformational, it will change people as well as systems (Albert, 1993).

> **Example:** The Chetwynd Project organizes a camp experi-
> ence for the community it works with. One woman tells of
> meeting another there, with whom she had a serious conflict.
> "We had a chance to get to know each other and talk about [the
> incident]. At the end of the week we could trust each other.
> Now, back in [the project], we look out for each other. We can
> work together."

Intra-Group Considerations

With equity as a base principle, and the notion of democratic organization development as a major theme, locality development's emphasis on co-operation and consensus becomes central. Consensus has three values for the community. First, it can facilitate a non-bureaucratic approach to community interaction (i.e., decision-making) and development. The assumption is that deciding issues in a non-bureaucratic manner can lead to the formation of more egalitarian institutions. Second, consensus can operate as a binding force for the creation of "solidarity" within the community. With its emphasis on listening, and the avoidance of winners and losers, it increases understanding and reduces barriers among members.[15]   Third, a consensus approach reflects what Staples (1984: 4) refers to as a necessary prerequisite for effective organizational development - "real faith in people's basic judgement, intentions, abilities, and instincts".

While consensus is essential, the use of conflict or contest strategies is also important. There will probably be situations where the membership includes intransigent, destructive elements which no amount of co-operation or consensus can change. Strategies that recognize and deal with the conflict situation should be developed.

Extra-Group Considerations

A community that seeks changes in the way elites deal with change will rarely be able to use consensus. Quite simply, the power-holders do not have the same interests or the same views as the community; and until they do − that is, when power is more equitably distributed − strategies of a contest nature will be necessary (Specht 1969).

In dealing with institutions, however, consensus orientation will sometimes be appropriate. There may be powerful institutions that are quite sympathetic to the aims of a disadvantaged group. For example, some Churches are quite progressive, and occasionally progressive political parties or unions can be sought as allies. The "Days of Action" in Ontario involved community groups, labour, and churches in confronting the Conservative government's repressive policies and actions. Indeed, as Moyer (1990) points out, we rarely try to directly change a powerful adversary. It is the wider public that we must "convince"; they will in turn force the adversary to alter its behaviour. It is important to be ready to listen, and to negotiate alliances that will further group interests. As a community is able to mount an effective campaign and power is achieved, an opposition will eventually have to be treated as an equal. In a sense, we use conflict strategies to obtain a situation in which equality is the basic condition for co-operation.

Reflection

Community development is about redistributing
power and resources.
It is a political process, not simply a tool or technique for
calming people or rubbing raw the sores of discontent.
—*Jim Lotz (1995)*

A major thrust of community organization must be to address the issue of power – the ability of people to affect their internal and external environments. This requires conceptualizing power and its elements, and focusing on coherent collective action. It also requires considerations of external and internal issues, and their dynamics. Finally, it is crucial that the people with whom we work are seen as victims of an unjust social/economic/political system, and as citizens with rights and abilities. This leads us to view community organization as a conflict- and consensus-oriented practice; which alerts us to the need to articulate objectives that are empowering, and oriented to progressive social change.

Endnotes

[1] For further discussion and more information regarding poverty see: Ross et al. (1994) The Canadian Fact Book on Poverty - 1994 (Ottawa: Canadian Council on Social Development).

[2] McDermott (1992) points out that neither the Canadian Human Rights Act of 1981, nor the Employment Equity Act of 1986, has resulted in any significant gains for women who continue to earn 35% less than male workers.

[3] The National Round Table on Aboriginal issues (1993) reminds us that Native Peoples occupy the bottom rung on the Canadian economic ladder — whether they live on reserves, in Métis settlements, or in urban centres.

[4]   A report published by the G. Allen Roeher Institute (1989) pointed out that Canadians who are disabled are poor. They tend to be unemployed or underemployed, but "most need to spend more money on items or services they require for daily living; and incur costs simply as a result of their disabling condition" (p.3).

[5]   For a more comprehensive and critical discussion of social structural issues, there are three books you may find useful: Ben Carniol's, *Case Critical* (Between the Lines Press); Ann Bishop's, *Becoming an Ally* (Fernwood Press); and Joan Kuyak's, *Fighting for Hope* (Black Rose Books).

[6]   Canadian Philip Rushton has put forward the theory that intelligence is related to race. The book, The Bell Curve, which draws in part on Rushton, recycles this discredited notion and adds its own. These are old ideas but still find an audience in North America.

[7]   Bandura's theory suggests that social change can be initiated from any of the three positions. One need not *feel* powerful to take powerful action; yet this very action will stimulate the self-perception of efficacy, as well as the material environment. The major difference is that the model in this book places more emphasis on the relationship between self-perception on the one hand; and the interaction of behaviour, environmental supports, and constraints on the other.

[8]   A most dramatic example of this effect can be found among torture victims (*Amnesty International Bulletin* December 1989/January 1990 Volume XVII, Number 1). A remarkably consistent set of symptoms can be found among victims of torture. Psychiatrists call it post-traumatic stress disorder; it affects combat veterans, victims of natural disasters - anyone who has been placed under **great stress in a situation they have been helpless to control**. (emphasis added)

[9]   Maier & Ellen (1965) refer to this as the principle of availability. The individual vents feelings (anger or fear or frustration) at whatever or whomever is available, rather than engaging in behaviour aimed at solving a problem or removing an obstacle. (pp. 100-101).

[10]   The framework that follows has been developed with three colleagues - Usha George, Susan McGrath and Ken Moffat - with whom I continue to work and learn.

[11] Since implementation of the "Freedom of Information Act", requests for information are often met with delays; and when documents are released they are often incomplete and censored. Government departments can ignore deadlines. Practically speaking, a successful complaint to the Information Commissioner often results in only sympathy and an acknowledgment that the department in question is in the wrong. (Webster, 1997)

[12] The British parliamentary system that allows a government to call an election at the most advantageous period for its re-election, provides a ruling party a power which further undercuts accountability to citizens. Wide use of polls and the ability to distribute government largesse provides more tools to increase its advantage.

[13] *The inclusion of belief as an element of power came out of conversations with community work activist and teacher Gupreet Malhatrah. My thanks to him.*

[14] As Alinsky has stressed, Lord Acton did not say that power corrupts but that it tends to corrupt. We cannot ignore power, or wish it away. As Joreen (1973) notes, power is always part of the equation. To try to deny it, and develop a "structure-less" organization, will only mean that we have to deal with power in an unclear and disabling manner. The point is, then, not to avoid power, but rather to have it clearly dispersed, so that all people are able to act upon their environments.

[15] See Hogie Wycoff's *Solving Problems Together* for a discussion of consensus decision-making techniques and their value.

2

OBJECTIVES OF A PRAGMATIC COMMUNITY PRACTICE

Unless we know where we want to go, we are in danger of ending up in the direction we are going.

—*Chinese proverb*

There are a variety of ways in which to define community organization practice. Some authors see it as planning and co-ordinating services to be more efficient and effective (Rothman and Tropman, 1987). Others see it as a means to redress power imbalances in society (Kahn, 1982; Rubin and Rubin, 1986). Still others see it as a means whereby community members more effectively share limited resources to create a better life (Ross, 1972; Biddle and Biddle, 1965). In a study by Lee (1988), a group of community workers were interviewed to determine how they articulated and understood the goals and objectives of their work. The conversations, analysis and reflection that came out of these interchanges led to the development of a practical - or pragmatic - down to earth model, of what community organization needs to strive for. Subsequently, additional community workers and activists have been interviewed[2]. These conversations and reflections have deepened our understanding, and have firmed up the elements in the model which is presented below. The model presented here sees community work as a means of addressing the goals of empowerment and social justice; as well as having five specific objectives: citizen involvement; sense of community; organization development; concrete benefits; and social learning. [3]

The Goal: Empowerment

Empowerment is a term that carries a number of meanings. Some see it as something we undertake. In this sense it is a process more that an outcome. Others see it as being rooted in what we can or cannot do. In this sense it is equated with actually having power. Community workers articulate the goal of community development as empowerment. (A goal is a generally preferred outcome that is expressed in terms that are global, and that carries with it a value orientation). Empowerment is understood by many community work practitioners as the sense in people that they have the ability and right to influence their environment. This definition is also reflected in much of community work literature. (Thomas, 1983) As such however, it is not precisely the same as possessing power. A person can have power but fail to realize it, and thus act in a disempowered manner[4]. That is, empowerment means that people have the feeling within themselves that they can act on their own behalf to be able to meet their physical, spiritual and psychological needs. Some, such as Gutierrez (in Checkoway, 1995), suggest that while "...empowerment is most often expressed as an increase in personal power, it tends not to distinguish the individual perception and actual increase in personal power; and tends not to reconcile personal and political power". It is suggested by others that the goal of empowerment is not individual, but multilevel; and as such, it is not sufficient to focus only on developing a sense of personal power in working toward social change - that efforts for change should include all three levels: individual involvement, organizational development, and community change (Checkoway, 1995). However, insofar as community work is oriented to empowerment, it can be seen to have a profoundly personal dimension.

Community Organizing Objectives

As well as this general personal goal, community work addresses specific outcomes or objectives that we can actually see in the communities within which we practice. They can be understood as the more concrete results that are expected to come out of a community development process. They have links to the more general concept –

the goal – to which they add concreteness, or an operational sense; and from which they draw direction and meaning. As well as speaking in general terms about power and empowerment, community workers wish to achieve important kinds of specific outcomes in and for communities. (These objectives are outlined below, and included in Figure 2-1: Community Organizing Objectives as Related to Empowerment).

1. Citizen Involvement or Participation

Nobody makes a bigger mistake than he who did nothing because he could do only a little.
—Edmund Burke

As Saul (1995) suggests, active citizenship is crucial to the health of any society. Participation means that we make decisions and act on them, in an attempt to do something about the problems that are important to us - "to help others while being helped [our]selves" (Rice, 1990: 9). Another way of saying this might be engagement in a change process - citizens actually acting on their own behalf to bring about some positive alteration in their environment. Saul (1995) makes the point that the very essence of citizenship is our active involvement in the life of our communities[1]. Citizens have both the right and the responsibility to act. To be able to act, however, people must see themselves as citizens; with rights and abilities to express opinions, and to acquire the resources they need. The link to empowerment is obvious: for a group of people to feel positive about their ability to influence their lives, they must actually take action. Simply "believing", like Peter Pan, will not make it so. If we never act we will never gain, and we will tend to lose the sense that we can act. Participation or action can be expressed at various levels: voting; attending a meeting; or joining a self-help, advocacy, social action group, for example. If people take up leadership responsibilities in community organizations, their participation deepens. The point of participation, however, is not simply leadership. It is **participation in action**. Action has a positive effect on how we see ourselves; and how other people see us, and/or the issues for which we advocate. Problems are often ignored when we are not active in bringing them before the public.

It is important, as Walter Bloomberger Jr. (1969) suggests, to promote collective as opposed to individual action. That is, widespread participation of the citizens in the attempted change process. Participation can be, and often is, a catch phrase that means both everything and nothing (Arnstein, 1969). The notion of participation for this book reflects four assumptions:

1.   The participation of the people must be meaningful, not token or simply for the benefit of decision making elites (Arnstein 1969).

2.   Decisions made with the serious and meaningful input of the people - who are both to be affected by them, and who implement them - will tend to be better, more realistic decisions.

3.   People who feel they have been part of a decision have more at stake in seeing the decisions implemented well.

4.   Participation of people in the decisions that influence their lives is healthy. People will tend to act better - more logically, sanely, and humanely - if they have a sense of influence over their lives.

2. Sense of Community

It's brought the community together. Before, no one got together much or knew each other. Its a real neighbourhood now - a community.
        —*Karen (Youth activist; Chetwynd Project, Jamestown)*

As we have seen in the previous chapter, community is a term which is used with a variety of meanings. We can speak of geographically-based groups like urban neighbourhoods. Community can also refer to people who share common attributes like race or culture. Whatever the bonding factor, however, it is important for the members to have a positive sense of themselves as a distinct group. There must exist a belief in the validity of their perceptions of their experience. Members must also possess a realistic satisfaction with their culture and traditions - not that these are superior to all others, but that they are valid and useful to them. Oppressed groups, such as Indigenous people in North America and Australia, invariably re-establish connections with their traditions and culture as a crucial part of their organizing. These are all important factors in overcoming the experience of victimization, and in establishing an image of themselves as people with a capacity and right to act.

We live in an alienating, and alienated, world dominated by technical efficiency and bureaucratic procedure (Rothman & Tropman, 1987). Boothroyd (1991: 84) puts it clearly:

> *The price we have paid for the material progress, personal liberty and cosmopolitanism enjoyed in [modern society] is a deep sense of aloneness, anxiety and impotence. This sense comes from the realization that ultimately only we or our immediate family cares about our economic fate, that our lives have no meaning outside that which we invest in them....*

The separateness that people feel not only leads to loneliness but also to feelings of confusion and impotence. Alienation is disempowering. We need solid social relationships. As lone (and alone) individuals we cannot hope to influence the powerful systems that exist all around us. Indeed, we may feel that they act on us in the most oppressive ways. To feel powerful we must also experience some connection to others. The rediscovery and re-establishment of a sense of community – our common experience, common dreams – can reduce the sense of powerlessness, and is a necessary component in any struggle to achieve social change.

3. Organization Development

> *You can have all the people on one side for whatever you want to do, but, unless they're organized, nothing will happen.*
> —*Chicago neighbourhood activist*

This category refers to the building of a new organization, or the improvement (for example, gaining resources, increasing participation) of an already existing one. A key element of power is having a large number of people on our side. Many writers (Rubin and Rubin, 1986; Alinsky, 1971), however, point out that numbers only lead to power when they are organized. An organized group stimulates energy in the form of cohesion and status. An organized people can share information (on the problems they face), resources, or their own skills. They can divide tasks, that need to be done to achieve their objectives, in an efficient manner. Further, the image of a strong community organization raises the status of the community in its own eyes, and often in those of the bureaucracies with whom it must deal (Alinsky, 1971). As noted in Chapter 1, there are difficulties associated with organization. Still, it is clear that for people to feel that they can achieve what they need, they must have an effective organization that can mount strategies over a significant time period.

4. Concrete Benefits or Resources

If I leave a community and people like me, and people have participated, and people feel good about themselves, that's important. But, if they have not achieved some good resource, well, I leave a failure.
—Barb Hanson, Toronto community worker

Community work often begins with the hope for the acquisition of: a specific resource; a right; an increase in service; or the development of a new facility of some sort (for example, a health care or recreation centre). As Thomas (1983) points out, there is a clear connection between lack of power and a people who are denied access to basic resources. Aside from the usefulness of the actual resource, community workers see a connection to empowerment. As one community worker put it, "people need victories to prove to themselves that they really are capable". It is much easier to believe in ourselves if we are part of a successful attempt to have a particular need met. If we understand that we have achieved one thing, we can believe that we can achieve others.

5. Social Learning

Social Learning, or local knowledge, is linked with the development of power - knowledge is one of the five elements of power. This objective has the following three facets:

(a) Skills - One refers to people in the community acquiring new skills. To know that we have the skills to accomplish something, that we are not simply wishing that we could do it, is a crucial determinant of our self image. People's feelings of self-esteem are often influenced by the realization that they have learned how to do something, such as: chair a meeting; write a news release; research some information; or deal with a bureaucracy or a complex situation. Community workers spend considerable energy helping activists as they learn how to operate their own organization, and develop strategies to influence "city hall" (Alinsky, 1971; Rubin and Rubin, 1986; Godard, 1991).

(b) System Knowledge - The ability to use the complex system of regulations, laws, and public organizations is important to our ability to influence our environment. It is something that all of us have to learn. As indicated in Chapter 1, information is often difficult to get or shrouded in technical jargon. Yet, with focused effort most of us can acquire the ability to negotiate these systems.

(c) Analysis - Social learning also refers to people gaining a new and useful analysis of themselves, their community, the larger society, and/ or the problems with which they are faced. As the Women's movement has demonstrated, having an understanding of the social, political, and economic factors that shape the conditions of our lives, can help to free us from self-blame and debilitating guilt over our inability to be as successful as we would wish (Adamson et al., 1989). To develop an active and healthy community we must have the opportunities, and means, to learn.

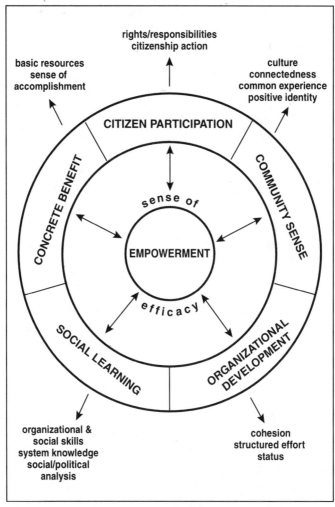

Figure 2-1   Community Organizing Objectives as Related to
Empowerment

Interrelationships Among Objectives

There are interrelationships among community development objectives. Participation can obviously be linked to the attainment of a concrete benefit, or the development of an organization. A viable organization, as we've noted earlier, is necessary to form the members of a community into a coherent force for the attainment of benefits. Social learning is a crucial element in that it stimulates and informs our actions as citizens. This objective is crucial to citizen involvement. Learning the workings of an organization, as well as the workings of the social-political environment, is required to make the organization successful. A positive sense of community identity can result from the successful work of its "own" organization. At the same time, the development of a sense of pride and of the connections among people should shape the nature of the organization, and provide a sense of vision for its work. The following description by Alinsky (1972) is a good example of the interrelationships among objectives:

> ...But perhaps our most important accomplishment...was intangible; by building a mass power organization, we gave people a sense of identity and pride. After living in squalor and despair for generations, they suddenly discovered the unity and resolve to score victories over their enemies, to take their lives back into their own hands, and control their own destinies.

It is important to be clear that the exclusive pursuit of a single objective would not be reflective of a community development process. Indeed, such a course of action might be harmful. For example, the development of a sound and efficient organization without reference to the objectives of community sense or citizen participation, can lead to power struggles, unnecessary internal conflict, elitism, and alienation of those not involved with the leadership. The temptation to formalize, or professionalize, an organization can lead to alienation of the community it was set up to serve (Cain 1993). Focusing solely on the acquisition of a concrete benefit can lead to co-optation - where people are "bought off" by some individual "goodie" that makes them feel they no longer need to struggle (Piven & Cloward, 1979). If we are only interested in one issue, a failure to achieve it may sap energy from carrying on with other objectives.

Social learning is crucial if we expect people to continue the struggle of development when the worker has left the scene. If we do not develop a critical analysis of what we are doing, what we are attempting to do, and the environment in which we are striving to do it, we will probably develop very naive strategies that could lead to defeat, disillusionment or co-optation.

Integration Of Empowerment And Objectives

Empowerment can be seen to exist when people believe that they possess the ability, and the right, to act effectively to influence their environments. To use Freire's (1970) language: a sense in people that they are subjects of the world rather than objects. It is clear, however, that empowerment is not something to be brought about in a simple way, or as something that can occur in isolation from concrete objectives. It emerges from, and contributes to, the objectives. It is both dependent on them, and energizes their achievement.

Empowerment in development is a complex phenomenon, something that must be examined critically, relative to its rootedness in the concrete experience of people. It has to be actualized through the achievement of specific objectives. In this sense, empowerment is something that informs objectives and tasks, and in turn is informed by them. The goal of empowerment - the feeling in people that they can influence their environment - is an intimate part of the objectives, and the objectives are intimate parts of empowerment. (See, once again, Figure 2-1). The concept of empowerment is not one of a state of mind that arrives after, or is caused by, the attainment of the objectives. Empowerment is reflected in, and experienced in, the actual achieving of the objectives; and the achievement of any of the objectives can be empowering.

Empowerment cannot exist outside of the striving. That is, as we begin to strive for the accomplishment of one or more of the objectives – as we find that we can participate in a discussion; or that by making our voices heard we begin to be listened to – we develop a sense that we have the ability to influence our lives. In this way, community development becomes "an empowering process"; the aim of which is to see people gain a greater sense of their ability to affect their environment. We can reflect on the success of community development projects by examining the extent to which there is evidence that any of the objectives are present, or are increased or decreased.

Community Work and Social Justice

Injustice anywhere is a threat to justice anywhere.
—Martin Luther King Jr.

Community workers, while focused on issues of a local or community-specific nature, must be very aware of the broader social and political context of the problems people face. Assisting a group to obtain a STOP sign, produce a community newspaper, develop a women's shelter, or get a regulation made less discriminatory, is important. On the other hand, none of these necessarily have the effect of eradicating, or even challenging, structural power imbalances. Adamson et al. (1989) point to the difficulty women activists face in trying to avoid institutionalization of their work. Indeed some authors (Mowbray, 1985; Repo, 1977; Mayo, 1975) claim that community workers actually contribute to the acceptance of society-wide oppressive systems by focusing on local or community-specific issues. Piven and Cloward (1979) worry that community workers will encourage people to organize when they should be pressing their demands for change. Most community workers, however, reject the notion that we are unaware of the potential for co-optation, or the "band-aid" nature, of our work. We tend to see our work as part of the patchwork quilt of action, and reflection, that can contribute to positive social change. Certainly no "revolution" is in sight. The promise of a truly egalitarian and empowering society seems to recede into the distance. Still, we need to remember the work of the social activists who have gone before us, leaving us a legacy of hope and some concrete changes that have clearly made the world a better place. Without the organizers in the Labour movement assisting in the struggle for decent working conditions in individual factories, workers would not have the benefits – safety standards and minimum wage legislation for example – they have today. Without the organizers in Feminist communities, women would be without many of the very important benefits – shelters, equal pay legislation – and services that exist today. The co-operative movement – housing, credit unions – owes its existence to the local struggles waged by its early organizers. In this way community organizing can be seen as an empowering process, and as a process of social change. Fromm (1966) reminds us, however, that social change is a slow process with radical improvements taking generations to achieve. We must be honest and clear about this. Those of us who involve ourselves in community work with the assumption that we will be involved in immediate fundamental change are sure to be disillusioned and will burn out very quickly. Acting on this kind of assumption will endanger the achievement of what is possible, and may indeed retard the struggle for long-term fundamental change.

On the other hand, what Alinsky (1971) has called a "realistic radical" - one who can approach the world the way it is and not the way one wishes it - can further the struggle by helping to establish powerful popular movements and organizations. It is important that community workers help the people with whom we work to reflect on how their particular struggle connects with the "larger" issues of the day - how the "local" strategy meshes with, or runs counter to, the flow of a "movement" (Moyer, 1990). It is equally important for community workers to help their groups look for coalitions so that they can become stronger, and the larger issues can be tackled when opportunities arise.

Social justice can be understood as a goal, like empowerment. However, while empowerment is a personal objective (an internal emotional and cognitive state in people), fundamental social change is found in the societal dimension. As with empowerment, social justice is a valued end state, difficult to define in concrete terms. Also like empowerment, it cannot be understood in isolation; it is only furthered in terms of the achievement of the development objectives in the community. Figure 2-2: Dimensions of Community Organizing, shows the interconnectedness of the three dimensions of community organization: the personal, societal, and community.

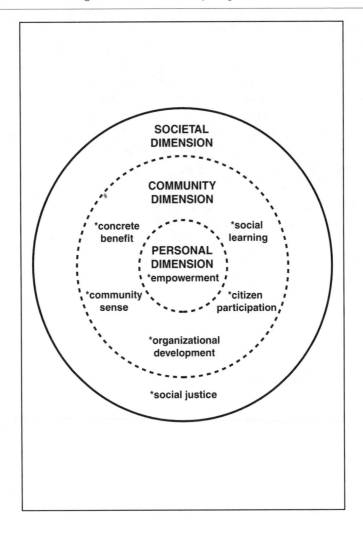

Figure 2-2: Dimensions of Community Organization

A Definition of Community Organization

Now that we have discussed the things that community workers are trying to achieve, we can try out a definition, and examine a few of its implications.

Community organization is a social intervention which seeks to maximize the ability of disadvantaged people to influence their environment, by developing power to: acquire resources; change inadequate institutions and laws; or build new ones, more responsive to their needs and those of all human beings.

Reflection

Community organization is an ancient, and persevering, human activity. In some ways it is the most natural of human activities – getting together to make necessary changes in the way we live together. At its best, it promotes equity, and liberation of our spirit of humanity. It is also, however, a time-consuming, threatening (to some) and very complex bit of business. It requires dedication, energy, and a rigorous analysis of situations, events, and people (from ourselves, as well as from those with whom we work). The rest of this book attempts to come to grips with the pragmatics of how our dedication is put into practice.

Endnotes

[1] For an interesting perspective on the connection between citizenship and empowerment see Kieffer (1984).

[2] The conceptions of the model have come out of discussion and reflection with community workers in Canada, Nicaragua, the U.S.A., Australia, Nigeria and Uganda.

[3] For other views and community work models see Checkoway's article (1995), "Six Models of Community", in (Community Development Journal, vol.30, n.1:2-19); or Rothman and Tropman's (1987) famous article, "Three Models of Community Organization Practice", in Cox et al. Eds., *Strategies of Community Organization* (F.E. Peacock Publishers).

[4] Michael Learner has written extensively on what he calls surplus powerlessness - the tendency to see ourselves as having less ability to influence our lives than we actually do. We can see how useful for it is for elites that the people buy into the notion that globalization, downsizing, and the triumph of technological change are part of "historical forces". To the extent we buy into this we acquire surplus powerlessness.

ROLES AND SKILLS IN PRAGMATIC COMMUNITY WORK

Right away I began to see that organizing was difficult.
It wasn't a party. I began to see all the things that he did,
and I was amazed - how he could handle one situation
and have a million things going in his mind at the same time.
                    —*Delores Huerta on Cesar Chavez (Levy, 1985)*

As indicated earlier, when we speak of a pragmatic model of community work we are talking about a melding of locality development and social action. Very simply the approach here is that the building of community capacity (developing and sharing resources, building consensus, etc.) cannot be undertaken without attention to issues of class, race, gender, etc.; as well as power and conflict - all social action concerns. The notions of role and skill then are based on this analysis of pragmatic community work. We work with people who we see as "victims" of an unjust social order; and as "citizens" with rights and responsibilities, and abilities to work for a just one. We are not able to do this unless we collaborate - work with the people as partners - in transforming the social reality in which we all live. To do this we must have some sense of what behaviors will be useful; i.e., what our role will be in the process.

The Notion of Role

Strean (1979) notes role can be seen from a number of perspectives. The one used here is that of "a synonym for behaviour." This is different from simply looking at activities, however, or a list of what workers might do. Rather it is a "pattern of behaviour" (Strean, 1979: 386).

That is, the key roles in community work will be discussed as sets of behaviours. But how is the idea of role useful to community workers? Very simply, if we see and understand that "role" is a set of particular behaviours it can provide us with a sense of the range of activities that we need to be prepared to undertake.

Two major points need to be made before the discussion of roles. First, no role can be thought of, or utilized, without reference to others. Second, all core roles imply the development of trust - they are part of a relationship that is built up through the enacting of each role (Jeffries, 1993). The five roles discussed here will be: initiator (catalyst/agitator); encourager/supporter; popular educator; mediator; and planner (strategist/advisor).

1. Initiator (Catalyst /Agitator)

People who are disadvantaged - particularly if they have been disadvantaged for a long time - often have become "stuck": either in inactivity (even apathy), or in repeated behaviours that are not getting them out of their predicament. (Remember "frustration instigated behaviour"). They may have all sorts of strengths and resources , but these can become dormant either in the face of serious, long term oppression (Kretzman & McKnight, 1993); or because they face sudden and complex threats to their living conditions (Ball, 1973). The situations of Indigenous people in North America or Australia, or of people in the "Black ghettos" of the U.S., fit the former dynamic. Various communities in Ontario that had to face the threat of local hospital closures are suggestive of the second. Thus, the community worker will often be required to assist community members in getting started - i.e., be the person who asks the first question or gets the first meeting called, etc.. The Social Work Dictionary (1991) puts it this way: "The social worker-community organizer's function of creating a climate of introspection and self-assessment for the...community, and facilitating communication, stimulating awareness of problems, and encouraging belief in the possibility change" (p.30). This initiator role is clearly central, and related to other key roles.

2. Encourager/Supporter

The community worker - because he is often working with people who have been deprived of the opportunity to influence their environments - will need to be able to encourage people to believe in themselves, their abilities, and their ability to learn. This has obvious connections with the catalyst role but is broader. Many times, as a community pursues its struggle, a worker will find people doubting themselves personally or as a collective. Dealing with this requires taking time to listen, and assuring those involved that they have been heard. It also includes validating the experience of the people that they have had disempowering experiences in the past. Organizers in the woman's movement provide lots of examples of this. It further involves assisting people in looking for and finding their strengths.

3. Popular Educator

As Colorado and Collins (1987), Illich (1972), and Freire (1970) have pointed out, education is a critical instrument or process that can be used for either subjugation or liberation. This is why the government and churches attempted for so long to deprive Native communities of their education function (Lee, 1992). The community worker's education role however, is not one of a formal teacher - where it is assumed that people are more or less empty vessels into which the bounty of knowledge is poured. Oppressed people have been taught to devalue their own experience and knowledge, and not to see the processes that have made them the objects of oppressive systems (Freire, 1970). Thus the community worker, as well as helping to provide new information and /or analysis, must often assist people to examine their old and new experiences so that they can identify: where the roots of problems lie; the things they know already; and what they need to learn in order to come together, and/or confront oppressive systems and processes.

Bill Lee facilitating popular education workshop with Northern Quebec Cree community workers.

4. Mediator

In western mainstream society we are encouraged to see each other as individuals first and people in relationships second. As Freire (1970) points out, we are taught (particularly where power and resources are concerned) that for one person or group to have more means that others must have less. This has clear ramifications for Native communities who have been stripped of many resources, and have little power at this time. Individuals, families, and groups then often wrestle for whatever resources and power that they perceive to exist within their borders. The resulting tension and conflict can be debilitating. Note the factions that we see in many Native communities, and in others such as women's groups and housing co-ops. Thus the community worker must at times play the role of mediator. The Social Work

Dictionary (1991) (unfortunately limiting it to family therapy) characterizes it thus: "...sometimes acts as a go between in getting various members of the [community] to communicate more clearly and fairly with one another" (p.141).

Mediation however, is actually far more complex then assisting people to communicate clearly to each other. After all, if we are clear in our communication we actually may be clear about how much we cannot stand each other. Mediation, at least in community work, must include assisting people to see, at best, their common humanity; or at least their common interests. Certainly that involves clarity, but it also involves reaching an understanding of their own legitimate needs as well as those of others. This does not necessarily mean that those involved must come to like each other - it is about working on building mutually respectful and trusting relationships.

5. Planner (Strategist/Advisor)

Strategy or planning requires a set of activities - research, issue identification, prioritizing. The worker - while looking to assist community members to understand their own strengths and identify targets for member action - must be clear that s/he brings a unique and valuable expertise to the community. One of these is the ability to plan a course of action, whether for internal development or external campaigning. This means that the worker must assist members to acquire these skills as well, of course. However, sometimes the best way to "teach" strategizing and planning is to be involved in a real process. Thus, initially, the community worker may have to take the "lead" in planning or strategizing, but in a collaborative manner in which people are able to learn to do it for themselves. As longtime organizer Mike Balkwill has stated: "That is what organizing is about - finding opportunity doorways, but not slipping through them alone. We have to build a path with others, so we can go through these doorways together". Again, there is a connection with other roles such as popular educator and catalyst.

Core Skill Requirements

We now turn to the area of the major or core skills that are called for when working within the pragmatic model of community organizing. What skills are required by the basic roles that have been described? While community work writers (Abrams et al., 1990; and Rothman and Tropman, 1987, for example) point out that the skills required are quite complex, there are some very important basic skills that are necessary for the community worker to have. Some are from the affective, or communication and interpersonal area (Kahn, 1994); others are more instrumental; while others are more political. Further, some will be more important to certain roles than others, but like much of community work these skills are pretty much interactive.

One last point is that, while we talk about skills as if they were single bits of ability, they usually require a number of interrelated behaviours. What is presented below is probably best understood as skill sets which include: listening; information gathering; analysis; facilitation; and negotiation. This can assist us in thinking about the broad core abilities that the basic roles require for useful intervention.

1. Listening

The ability to listen to community memebers - to hear what they are really concerned about, and the emotion with which they say things - is a crucial skill, and basic to any social work. It is particularly important when working with those who have a long history of not being listened to, or of being discounted. As such, there is no role that does not require the worker to be a good listener. If, for example, one is going to initiate reflection, or action, or encourage people, appropriate listening is crucial. A mediator must be able to understand both sides of a dispute in order to be able to frame an appropriate and useful intervention.

2. Information Gathering

Information gathering - about the community, individuals, or issues, for example - is also basic. While it may have less relevance to the encourager/supporter role, it will be used in others. Information is like energy - a source of power which fuels one's activities in getting things started and in strategizing. A popular educator needs basic information to help people structure their learning experiences. A mediator must have information about the basics of the situation, and about the history of a dispute.

3. Analysis

Analysis is the ability to take information and make connections or put it together in some meaningful whole or picture. It is the creation of meaning out of separated parts. The ability to analyse situations and problems is key to three of the roles: popular educator, mediator and strategist. The popular educator is someone who assists people to develop their own meanings out of their own experiences. The mediator must help people find their common interests within what may appear to be a very fractured community relationship system. The strategist / planner must be able to help people build a coherent picture of their situation and their options.

Community worker Janet Fishlock listening to community concerns about the lack of water in a Northern Nigeria village.

4. Facilitation

Facilitation is defined here, very simply, as: the ability to assist a group to achieve a purpose through working together. The worker is not doing the groups's work, but acting in a manner that helps them do it well. This may involve: helping set up meetings and agendas; or encouraging participants to listen carefully to each other at a meeting; or supporting a leader who is chairing a first meeting. Much of the work of community development is based on productive and smoothly functioning groups, so facilitation can be seen as basic to all the community development roles.

5. Negotiation

Negotiation is bargaining in order to assist people to attain some form of benefit, or to resolve a dispute. Negotiation may take place within the community, between two groups that see their needs or interests differently. In this case it is a skill likely used in relation to the mediator role. The worker is more or less disinterested (not on one side or the other) and assists people in coming together in order to find their commonalities. On the other hand, negotiation is a skill required when representatives of the community are attempting to gain something from an outside body; the worker is likely playing the role of strategist/ planner: the worker is on the side of the community people, using negotiation abilities to help the community achieve its goals.

Reflection

It is useful to make a couple of observations as we leave considerations of roles and skills.

Being Self-aware[1]

These roles and skills are ones basic to community organization; but they are not the only ones a worker will require. We always need to be prepared to reflect on our abilities in order to grow, and to improve ourselves. As well as understanding the various contexts that surround our work, we must have a handle on what we are about – our own values, biases, analyses.

The worker is not merely a programmed automaton. We take on, consider, react to, and discard any number of values and perspectives that we meet with as we grow and develop. What is important is to understand how we see and understand the world - not so as to force it on others, or to keep it from contaminating them - but so that we can be clear, honest, and direct when we are doing things. If we don't know how we see things (and obviously this can and will change with experience) it will be hard to answer the questions that people invariably ask: "What the hell are you here for?"; " What is your stake in this?". As Bishop (1994) notes we all occupy different points on the various continuums of privilege. As well, we have all been touched by racist, homophobic, or sexist ideas. None of us is perfect, and part of ourselves may be working on this stuff for a long time. We have to possess some self-knowledge - what things bother us, motivate us, make us angry or sad. We don't want emotional imperatives to motivate our reactions to people and situations.

By being clear and honest with ourselves we are in a position to be more pro-active with the people with whom we work. For example, if an organizer understands that he has a need to be personally very well-organized, he is less likely to see that attribute as absolutely necessary in others. Or, if he is aware that it has taken him effort and time to be able to confront difficult people, he will more likely be able to demonstrate patience with his community members as they struggle to develop the skill. We will be more comfortable in making demands of people, and encouraging them, if we know that we are not doing so out of some personal need or bias of our own, but because of their needs and those of the situation. Understanding ourselves also includes being aware of what we are good at and where we have to improve. This keeps us from getting into situations that are over our heads, and assists us in knowing when to ask for help. Ultimately it will help us to be more secure.

Diversity Issues and Being an Outsider

Earlier it was mentioned that community organization is often practiced by people from outside of the community (Cruikshank, 1990). Sometimes that simply means that we don't live in the same community. Increasingly, however, we will probably find ourselves working with people who are of a different culture then we are, or have profoundly different life experiences than ourselves (Narayan, 1994). We may have ways of seeing situations, or of communicating, which are different from those of the people we are working with. This will impact on how (and whether) we take on different roles, or use skills. For example, it can be tricky for a white person who is attempting to play the role of advisor to a Native group, who may be somewhat sensitive to the issue of "advice giving" (given the paternalism many Native people have experienced from members of the dominant society). A similar dynamic can exist in situations where males are working as advisors among women.

> **Example:** A community worker with an Australian develop-
> ment organization was stationed in the small South Pacific
> nation of Vanuatu. Her first assignment was to give some work-
> shops to local women on how to conduct meetings. She was
> worried that this might appear presumptuous, but was not sure
> she could confront the funder at such an early time in the project,
> and did not feel that she could turn down the opportunity. Her
> strategy was to emphasize the popular education role. She
> facilitated the sessions in a way that encouraged the women to
> reflect on how they were running their meetings already. Oc-
> casionally she would raise questions that assisted them in re-
> flecting on how they could improve things. The development
> organization was happy that the event had taken place, and the
> women were very pleased with the process and with what they
> had learned.

A similar issue can exist in relation to communication. Hall and Hall (1987) make the point that some cultures (Euro-North American for example) are contractually oriented. That is, there is a tendency to want our working relationships to be very clearly spelled out - very "product oriented". Efficiency is valued, and a preference for written contracts. Other cultures (First Nations might be an example here) tend to prefer the work relationship to grow out of personal relationships. There is less dependence on contract, and more on understanding where people are coming from and who they are as people. Process tends to be more valued than efficiency or strict rules.

Now clearly these are generalizations. Native people and women are not automatically going to reject advice from a white male. Neither First Nations people or women are automatically going to reject advice from a white male. And First Nations folks understand the nature of the world they live in and the utility of having written contracts. Being born into a culture does not necessarily mean that one will not take on attributes of others with which we come into contact. Many Euro-North Americans can be very concerned about and adept at relationship building for example. The point here is not to put forward "cultural laws", but to suggest that we need to think about how different groups might respond to different roles, and how skills may have to be tailored to unique situations. An important rule in community work is to never take anything for granted, but let our actions emerge out of our experience and reflection.

While there are particular challenges and struggles to being an outsider, there are also important positive aspects:

a. Fresh Perspective

The outsider may bring some fresh perceptions and thinking to situations. As long as we are respectful of people's experience, this can be a valuable asset to a community. An outsider can ask those "dumb" questions that insiders may not think to ask because they are so deeply involved in the issues.

> **Example:** A female Native community worker tells the story of going into a small community, and quickly realizing that the reserve was being run completely by men. In going around

the community she was told about how the women felt shut out and disrespected. The women kind of deputized her to raise the issue at a Band Council meeting. She was nervous about doing this, but felt she had built some trusting relationships among the councilors. She decided to do it by asking the men why no women were on council, or in any leadership positions in the community. While there was some (not unexpected) resistance from some of the men, the majority found that it was an interesting issue. One pointed out that traditionally women had occupied places of respect in Native communities. This was the start of a process, not always an easy one, that brought more women into leadership roles in the Band.

b. Perception of Impartiality

As suggested above, communities often find themselves dealing with splits and alignments within their membership. A community organizer from the outside may be seen as someone who is not connected to one group or another, and be more able to bring people together in an atmosphere of safety.

> **Example:** A worker (non-Native) was hired by a Native community which had an acknowledged history of factional conflict. As part of building a community analysis, he facilitated a series of popular education workshops. Representative people from different factions were brought together to work on a coherent community vision, and to identify some of their key problems. At the end of each two day session they held feedback rounds to evaluate the process. In every case participants talked about how nervous they were in coming to the sessions, and how important it had been to have an outside person there as a guide. They also spoke of how good it felt to hear some of the "different ideas" in the community, and to be able to express their own.

Being an outsider is a difficult position to negotiate (Cruikshank, 1990). It brings pitfalls, stress and opportunity. It is important to be aware of

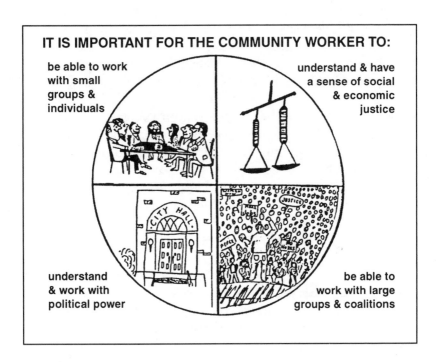

these, and not to try to be perfect. We are going to make mistakes. If we know this, and know that we are not the only ones to face these dilemmas, we may be able to take these opportunities to grow and develop as community workers.

Endnote

[1]   Katrina Shields offers some useful perspectives on the use of self in *In the Tiger's Mouth* (1994; New Society Publishers); and Len Desroches (1996) provides a useful tool for self-reflection with his work, *Allow the Water* (editions DUNAMIS publishers).

SECTION II

Phases of Community Organization

PHASES OF COMMUNITY ORGANIZATION

The community work process will be divided into phases (see Figure II). These phases, on paper, look like clearly separate aspects of the work. They are used here, however, as a way of talking about the variety of issues and tasks that are important to achieving the objectives of community development. In reality, many phases will overlap and integrate with others.

For example, development of a community analysis process will contribute substantially to the creation (or re-creation) of an organization. The same is true of popular action. Evaluation may go on formally at various times in the life of a community project. On the other hand, the people involved will constantly be reflecting on (evaluating) the things in which they have been involved – meetings, actions, negotiations – so that they can repeat the good things and eliminate unsuccessful behaviours. This being said, we begin this section by examining the issues and tasks in the first phase of organizing, Pre-Entry. (At the end of each chapter, you will find a chart that summarizes the key aspects of each phase).

PHASE	DESCRIPTION
PRE-ENTRY	Contract with the Sponsoring Body(s) *The politics of getting hired and creating a realistic description of objectives*
CONTACT / ENGAGEMENT	Learning about the community and vice-versa *The progress and politics of being accepted by the community and beginning to build clear expectations of each other*
COMMUNITY ANALYSIS	Community image building *Identifying action issues* *Beginning the community organization*
ORGANIZATION/ DEVELOPMENT	Building the organization and establishing good working relationships
POPULAR ACTION	Keeping the organization going *Development of strategies for change*
EVALUATION	Who, What, When, Where, How and Why? What next?
ENDING	Saying goodbye Letting the people say goodbye Letting them get on with their work

Figure II: Phases of community organization

4

PRE-ENTRY

As an organizer I start from where the world is, as it is,
not as I would like it to be.
That we accept the world as it is does not in any sense
weaken our desire to change it into what we believe it should
be - it is necessary to begin where the world is if we are
going to change it to what we think it should be.
—Saul Alinsky (1971)

Most of the time, community organizers are not hired directly by the people they are supposed to help organize. Communities which are in most need are usually the least likely to be able to afford the "luxury", or even to see the need for hiring an organizer. A public institution (like a government department) or a private one (such as a church group or a foundation) may do the initial thinking, advertising, and hiring. Kramer (1970: 222) makes the point that: "Formally, the sponsor serves as the legitimizer and sanctions his change agent role". Even when community leaders do the hiring, many of the issues raised here will be relevant. Leaders are not always well connected to the people. As well, leaders are often using dollars from outside - government, foundations, church groups for example - and this will impact on the nature of the development program for which they are hiring.

It is crucial that the potential organizer gain a clear and definite contract with the hiring/funding body. Further, it is important for the potential organizer/employee to understand the sponsor, the sociopolitical context, their structural interrelationships, and the ways in which they can affect the objectives, methods, roles, and outcomes of the organizing endeavour (Kramer, 1970).[1]

If there are people within the organization who are cool to the project, or to some of its objectives; or are even merely ignorant of the community organizing process, the worker can end up spending a great deal of time later on having to educate people, or on mending fences. We have to learn whom the internal advocates of the program are, and (as much as possible) leave them with the responsibility for handling organizational questions. If this responsibility for keeping her organizational base strong is left vague, or solely with the organizer, she has to divide herself in two - half for the community, half for the funding organization - in order to maintain her credibility with the latter. With these questions on the table, the worker can make some decisions about how (or if) to proceed; and, at the very least, the potential for unforeseen events may be decreased.

Internal Political Situation

It is a good idea to try to establish contacts within the funding/sponsoring organization so that we can gain the most realistic perspective possible. These are a few of the initial questions we should be asking:

- Who, in the funding/sponsoring organization, is advocating the program?
- What is their status?
- Do they have good links to the community?
- Who, in the funding/sponsoring organization, is resistant to the program?
- Why, and for how long?
- What is the status of the person resisting the idea? It is important to know whether this is someone who is "noisy" but not influential, or a person whose "yes" or "no" can make a real difference.

External Political Situation

What kind of credibility or clout does the funding organization wield in the larger community? What kind of credibility or clout does the organization wield in the particular target community (for example: an urban Native population, a certain neighbourhood, or a group of disabled people)?

> **Example:** It is no secret that many Canadian institutions have historically had a destructive record in First Nations communities. This is particularly true of the Department of Indian Affairs (DIA), and the churches who were involved in the residential school system.. It is important that a person wanting to do development work in these communities be aware of how individual communities, or organizations, feel about accepting money or other resources from such mainstream institutions. Many refuse, because of the institution's records, to accept funding from DIA (for example, the First Nations journal "Beedaudjimowin") or from churches (a southern Ontario Native organization was offered the use of a local church hall, however, they could not accept the offer because many community members, had experienced the residential school system themselves or through family members, were outraged and refused to attend events held there). On the other hand, there are Native communities which are working closely with churches, and using these institutions' resources to develop healing programs and in their own communities' social justice initiatives.

Therefore, it is important to be aware of the particular political situations and feelings of the particular community one is working with at any given time.

Who, or what, does the organization represent? For example, who is involved on its board or policy-making body? This question can be related to the first two - persons possessing power in the overall community, and in the organization, might have little or even negative influence within the target community and vice-versa.

Are there groups or institutions that are likely to resist efforts at change relative to the target community? How powerful are these groups?

Does the sponsoring body have particular enemies within the proposed target community, or the community at large, that tend to react negatively to any change thrusts mounted by the sponsoring body?

- What are the dynamics involved?
- Are they based on personalities, or principles?
- What is the history of the conflict? What were the major events? Who were the major players?
- What are the prospects for resolving the enmity?
- If no resolution is in sight, what other possibilities exist for dealing with the problem?

> **Example:** The Chetwynd Project, in Toronto, follows Alinsky's principle of requiring an invitation from the communities with which it works. Part of the selection process is to sort through those applications received, for those which seem the most appropriate. Recently two communities applied. While both seemed to be ones which could benefit from development intervention, one had supporting letters from two major social agencies, while the other did not. (Both agencies had extensive involvement in the two communities). This was significant in that Chetwynd depends on the cooperation of agencies for its work. The staff had to ask whether there was a message here: that the agencies would not be cooperative unless "their" choice was selected; or was it simply that the other community had not asked for the agencies' support? The staff also wondered if the one community wished to have nothing to do with these two powerful agencies. Whatever the answers here, it is important to get good, clear information, so that no nasty surprizes come up that may damage the work being done.

Sponsor's Ultimate Interest

What is the **ultimate interest or goal** of the sponsoring body in having this particular community become organized?

- To get people to utilize the services of the funding body more fully?
- To create a new and better image of itself within a certain segment of the population; i.e., P.R.?
- To get in on the latest fad? Though many governments in North America are touting the John McKnight (1995) idea - that the community is the best place to handle social problems - unfortunately there is little commitment to the necessary level of funding.
- To tap some new money that has appeared on the funding horizon? Though government funding levels have decreased, certain areas might have money on a project basis. For example, disability rights education has been identified as an important issue in some parts of Ireland. (Thanks to the organizing of disability activists).
- Altruism or ideology? Are those advocating the project interested in empowerment and social justice?
- What are their critiques of poverty or racism, for example?
- Anything else we may think that is relevant to the particular sponsor and/or community ?

Sponsor's Concrete Objectives

Does the sponsoring body have a clear, and definite, conception of what the "organized" community might actually look like - an informed and active citizenry, or simply a program with a nominal community board? Is there an interest in really developing the community? (Remember empowerment, and social justice, and the five objectives). How influential have community voices been in creating the picture? How rigid a mandate will the organizer be given, and how does that fit with your own principles and style?

It is important to have clearly defined expectations in order to avoid misunderstandings or arguments, which could sap time and energy at a later more crucial time.

Taboo Issues

Are there **special issues** that the sponsoring body will not want the organizer to touch? If so:

- What are they? For example, are there any subtle messages that diversity issues should be played down?
- How public is the organization about this?
- To what degree is this stand congruent with the stated mandate of the organization? For example, one would expect that a Roman Catholic funding body would object to pro-abortion involvement. On the other hand, objection to involvement in anti-land development activities would not appear logical - though it might exist for other, less public, political reasons.
- Why does it want these issues avoided? What relationship do these issues have to the organization, to members of its board, or to its funders?

    Example: A social planning council in a major Canadian city has, over the course of the last 30 years, often run into trouble with its major funder, the United Way (McGrath, 1998). The latter, dominated by large corporate interests, objects to the council becoming involved with rigorous policy advocacy. When the Council becomes too "radical" the United Way has invariably tried, often successfully, to move it back into a less controversial line.

- How does this stand fit with our own value position? This may require some careful thought and self-evaluation. (Remember our discussion of the importance of being self- aware - Chapter 3). It is dangerous to avoid dealing with an uncomfortable fundamental question at this point. Trying to figure things out in the heat of the moment can drive us crazy and/or lead to indecisive and ineffective action.

- Is the stand of the organization negotiable?
- What about our own stand?
- Any other possible reason? Think about it.

Taboo People or Institutions

If contest situations develop, are there special people or institutions that the sponsoring body will demand that we or our group not confront (e.g., social agencies with financial or legislative ties to our outfit, or companies who have contributed to the coffers of the sponsoring body)? Alternatively, are there folks who are expected to be kept out of the organizing project?

> **Example:** A coalition of community agencies came together to raise concerns about their regional government's approach to welfare recipients, and some very harsh new measures that were being instituted. A couple of workers were mandated to do the research, and a group was organized to make a strong presentation before regional council. The issue got some great coverage in the local media. After the presentation, the workers started to get pressure from one of the major community agencies to stop the project, or at least soften it considerably. It turned out that board members of that agency had some serious political ties with some of the councillors, and were uncomfortable at seeing "their friends" (who could probably help them at fund raising time) suffer any embarrassment.

- Who are they?
- Why are these people special - positively or negatively - to the funding body?
- Are there organizational interrelationships?

These questions may not always be easy to answer, and we are not suggesting that we need to become investigative reporters. On the other hand, it does make sense to look at the various "boards of directors" (in both the business and the voluntary sectors) and see what overlap exists. Talk to friends in the area, look through relevant documents, and try to get a sense of these "policies".

Time Frame And Funding

Is there a guarantee of funding for the total projected period?

- What time period does the funding cover? Is there a projected time span for the project (which may in fact reflect the funding body's conception of "the organized community", or its ultimate goal - see above).
- Are the funding and time frame realistic? People often believe that things can be achieved far more quickly then they can. Remember, community is complex and so is community work. It takes time.
- Can this time frame be elongated later - is there a provision for the project to be renewed or extended?

It is worth considering Piven and Cloward's assertion that the majority of citizens' organizations will receive continued funding not because they fulfill a primary need for people, but because they have a payoff for the elites (1977, xxi). Of course, the needs of one are not always diametrically opposed to the other. Kramer (1970: 223) suggests that it is legitimate for organizational needs and interests to be accorded some recognition. Still, it is an important caution for an organizer to keep in her head when considering continued funding.

Is There a Definite End to the Project?

There are some groups that have successfully planned and campaigned over the years to maintain their funding and thus their lives, eventually to become organizations without a foreseeable end. The problem is that a lot of energy and creativity has to go into the fight to keep them alive - energy which might have been better utilized to carry out their mandate. On the other hand, very few projects ever will be funded "for life." Really understanding the ideas about the time frame of the funder at the beginning makes it easier to strategize extending a project's life if it becomes logical and necessary to do so. It is important to remember that community development is a process. The dividends usually do not come early. In the world of commerce, good companies will invest resources over a number of years before expecting a return on their investment. This is one area in which we should follow a "business" model. We need to consider the results of community work more in these terms. If we expect quick results, we may be setting our communities, and ourselves, up for failure. This may lead potential funders to cynicism and negative reaction.

Take some time to think and talk about the time frame in terms of what has to be done. If it appears to be unreasonably short, we should ask ourselves:

- Can it be lengthened? If so, how? If not, why?
- Is the funder expecting quick results? Often it is.
- Does it have any understanding of the process? Often it has only a limited one.
- Is education needed?
- Does this reflect a fad which may fade in a year?
- Is there any way of negotiating a compromise?
- Is there provision for lead time? (See below)

If it can be done, it is a good idea to negotiate sufficient lead time (See Chapter 5: "Contract and Engagement Phase") to "de-cobweb" our own brains - that is, to get rid of any pre-conceived ideas of the target community, and begin to gain an understanding of what it's really like. (The importance of reflecting on our pre-conceived ideas can be appreciated if we remember our discussion of our being "outsiders" in the communities we are often working with - see Chapter 3). Paulo Freire states the case nicely: "One cannot expect positive results from an education or political action program which fails to respect the particular view of the world held by the people. Such a program constitutes cultural invasion, good intentions notwithstanding" (1970: 84).

This does not mean that we must strip ourselves of personal beliefs and values - but that the community must be seen through the context of the lives, situations, and consciousness of the citizens we will work with (Alinsky, 1971: 70).

Accountability

Accountability refers to who has the right and power to ask questions, demand answers, and evoke sanctions regarding the quality, effectiveness, and relevance of your service or practice, and the method of delivery.

* How much of the organizer has the funder bought? To whom do they think we are accountable? Or do they really see the money as buying the organizer for the community? Again, it is a matter of values and consistency. If we believe that power relationships need to be altered, it would be a bad precedent to have a project where the organizer's ultimate accountability lies outside of the community she is organizing.

* Ideally, the funding should go through the group to which the organizer will relate. In some cases, however, the community is not sufficiently "together" to be able to apply for and administer funding for the employment of an organizer (at least not at first). A good question to consider would be: "How soon does the sponsoring group see the structure of financing being altered"?. Many funding or sponsoring agencies - given a basic bureaucratic distrust of non-hierarchical control, and perhaps of people in general - may cast a jaundiced eye on any such funding transfer. For example, it took one community worker, her supervisor, and her community in Toronto over three years to convince her agency that the community organization could be entrusted with the funds to actually hire her itself. Approximately one year after that, the sky had not only **not** fallen, but the people in the organization began thinking about how they might eventually be able to survive, and do well, without the community worker at all. In another two years the worker was able to leave a strong viable organization standing on its own.

- In cases where the organizer is being sent to "develop" a role, the issue of accountability transfer (from the funding source to the community) must be thoroughly hashed out, understood, and agreed upon. Obviously the role to be developed cannot, and should not, be completely predicted or predetermined. However, there needs to be a clear sense of what the organizer's parameters are, while at the same time an assurance that not too many options are closed off.

- At times it may make sense to have accountability within the sponsoring institution spread around (or spread among various sponsors). This allows for some protection for the community and the organizer in that no one person can exercise the power of life or death over the project.

Example: A small social planning council in southern Ontario has managed to get funding from three United Way organizations, as well as from their regional government. When the region objected to some of its action research in the community, the council was able to rally the other funders to its position. The region backed out of its objections.

The less positive side of this approach is that it increases the number of people we must keep informed. On the level of multi-institutional funding, it can rob the organizer of valuable time that gets siphoned off into fund-raising, reports, and other administrative necessities.

Example: A neighbourhood organizing project in Toronto had a number of funders - child welfare agencies, parks and recreation department, and the social housing authority. There was often confusion around goals, and how much funding each agency would provide. Ultimately, the project consolidated its funding, and now feels more secure.

Evaluation

This is an issue linked strongly to accountability, as well as to concerns of productivity and efficiency. Data gathering and reporting should be planned flexibly so that they can be of use to the community. Evaluation should be built in from the moment a project is conceived. The original objectives should be clear, and accounting and statistical procedures should be in place. More will be said about this in Chapter 9, but it is worth mentioning at this point that the timing of evaluation should be related to the process of organizing.

- Who does the evaluation: is it community self-evaluation; the sponsor; staff; or is it contracted out to someone else?

- To what extent will the funding body, the general community and the community organization be involved:
  - In the data gathering?
  - In the formation of the questions?
  - In the consideration and analysis of data?
  - Sharing in the formation of strategies?

- When will it be done? How often?

- Is the evaluation seen as an integral part of the total community development program? Is it action-oriented? Can the process itself assist the community to identify and clarify objectives? (see above)

- Is there funding provided specifically for the evaluation (and for the needs that cannot be specifically planned for, e.g., training)?

Reflection

These questions suggest that a lot of work is required during this phase. We may already have a good idea about the answers to some of them. As well, we may find some of greater interest (e.g., having a particularly strong value stance) while others may be less important.

If the pre-entry phase is completed positively, we are in a good position to present ourselves, and our overall task, to the community. This is all that a well accomplished pre-entry can do – it offers no particular expectation for succeeding with the community. It will not keep surprises (good or bad) from occurring. On the other hand, a well-founded contract with the funding body does two important things:

- Limits unexpected behaviours by the sponsors and the organizer.
- Provides the organizer, sponsor, and ultimately the people of the community with a foundation and framework within which to discuss the contentious issues which invariably arise in any change process.

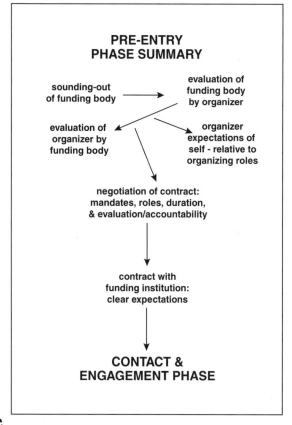

Endnote

[1] Ben Carniol's *Case Critical* 3rd. Ed. (1995) offers a solid critique of the way in which social agencies can constrain work for social change.

Chapter

5

CONTACT
AND
ENGAGEMENT

*Intervention that is defensible on ethical grounds must
always be paradoxical. One acts for others only to the point
of initiating a symbolic gesture of genuine concern and
respect. This is the first overture. There is further action if,
and only if, the other responds positively. The response is
much more than consent as we usually think of consent.
After this accepting response a spiral of action, reaction, and
interaction can result between the two. In the final act of
love, who is to say who [is] the helper and who the helped?
The notion of help is finally irrelevant.*
—R.A. Sim (1969) in Lotz, 1995

The first thing any potential organizer must do to try to engage a
community is **establish contact**. There are two fundamental ways in
which to do this. First, if the community is already somewhat cohesive
- and has some sort of formal or even informal leadership - we can
make contact with that leadership. For example, if workers are
attempting to organize themselves at their workplace, the organizer
might first approach the people who have the most visibility and
apparent credibility. If a worker is being hired by a housing co-operative
there will already be a board of directors running things. Of course, if
a community is already organized in some fashion the worker may be
invited in by the leadership. For example, a housing co-operative may
be looking for an organizer to assist the community to deal with some

internal strife and/or increase participation, etc. In these cases many of the same questions raised in Chapter 4 should be addressed.

Second, where the community appears to be unorganized (for example, around environmental concerns), or where there is little information (we may be asked to go into an area where there is a high rate of vandalism to see if we can assist a teenage population to organize and channel itself into constructive change), a good deal of low-key familiarizing may be necessary until credible, or relevant, people appear. In a geographical community this may take the form of walking around the area, or establishing oneself in places like restaurants, taverns or shopping centres frequented by community members.

> **Example:** Two workers were hired by a group of First Nation agencies to do some action research with Native people living on the street. They mapped out where they would find people - drop-ins, shelters, and popular street corners. Then they went out and started talking to people.

If there is no centrality to the community (like a social housing development, for example), it may simply be a matter of door-knocking or phoning. This is done until we achieve a sense of the people, and hopefully discover some informal leadership. Then, more formal contact can be made. Nicholas von Hoffman (an Alinsky organizer in Chicago) gives some of the feeling of the contact and entry phase:

> *"I learned more during those weeks than I ever learned in my life. I really think I did. It was day after day of going out and finding out about other people and other things, taking it home, putting it down, thinking about it, trying to make sense out of it. Day after day after day, making the connections and trying to understand people's motives and activities. I cannot think of anything I have ever gone through that was more valuable."*
> *(Horwitt, 1989: 276)*

However an organizer decides to make contact, there are questions and principles that should be kept in mind.

Introductory Questions

What is the image, if any, of the funding body in the community? Often an agency will have a long history of intervention with a particular group. This reputation will influence the initial attitudes of members to the introduction of an organizer funded by it.

> **Example:** A Canadian-funded, university-sponsored water project in northern Nigeria hired a couple of community workers to do a small survey in the target village. They were to get some basic demographics, and attitudes toward the proposed intervention (which was to assist the people in sharing knowledge about the use and storage of water in times of drought). One of the first things the workers discovered, however, was that there was cynicism and distrust of the project. This stemmed from two dynamics. First, government and university officials had been coming to the village for years promising assistance with water and electrification. They had asked a lot of questions, had gotten a lot of data for themselves, but had done nothing. None of the workers in the current project had any connection with what had gone on before, but the information turned up by the workers suggested the need to slow down the project and spend some time gaining trust in the village.

Members of Jos University Community Water Project Team chat informally with villagers.

What is the image, if any, of community workers? Have there been bad, or good, experiences in the past that will influence community attitude? Some disadvantaged communities, for example, have been so "used" by researchers and student social workers (counselors and organizers) that any outsider coming in has to live down a great deal. On the other hand, a bad intervention image can be used by people who want to resist change, or who wish to guard their own advantaged position. It is tough for an organizer (and ultimately the organization with which he's connected) to always have to fight a rear-guard action against a negative image not of his making.

> **Example:** A co-op housing project was having difficulty in getting itself organized. Members were particularly concerned with a lack of participation. Unfortunately, one of the high profile members had had a bad experience with a very new CD worker some years previously in another co-op. Thus, he was extremely suspicious of the community worker who was hired to assist the co-op. The fact that he wished to maintain his own power on the Board of Directors was also a factor - he didn't relish people participating in a way that would make him more accountable to the residents. For some time he was able to frustrate the work of the organizer by linking her activity with the legitimate concerns about the person he had known several years previously.

Are there aspects of the community that require particular attention? Are there particular experiences or attitudes in the community which we should be prepared to deal with? Some communities (because of the experience of their members, or attitudes related to ethnic tensions) have particular issues that a community worker will have to be cautious of, and which will frame what she does as she seeks to make contact.

> **Example:** A worker was beginning her work in a large non-profit housing project in Mississauga, Ontario. The board of directors of this building had sent a flyer to all tenants introducing her, and indicating that she would be knocking on doors

to introduce herself personally. The great majority of the tenants had come from Croatia in the former Yugoslavia and their first language was not English. Fortunately the worker had a chance to examine the flyer before it was sent. Being somewhat familiar with eastern European languages, she checked it over and found it was written in a Serbian dialect. This would have been a terrible beginning for her as some Serbs and Croats had imported their disputes to Canada. This would have made people quite distrustful. She got a Croat friend to translate the flyer into the appropriate dialect. Matters were even more complicated - she was of Ukrainian descent and she had a name that looked like it might be Serbian. Again this would have caused initial distrust. She solved this problem by making it a point to speak some Ukrainian to people as she did her door knocking.

Principles to Guide Engagement

The organizer, from the moment of first visibility, is modeling his future behaviour to the community. As Speeter (1978: 21) says "You as an organizer will be looked upon as model communicator, co-worker, and risk-taker, whether you want that or not". Winning trust is very important here. The organizer must be prepared to begin immediately to demonstrate personal qualities and skills of confidence, tact, empathy, ability to listen, and accountability. The principle of **beginning where the people are** is crucial (Alinsky, 1971). Their value system must be quickly learned, and respected, so that we can dialogue with them (Freire, 1970).

There is no rule that dictates that the organizer must approve of each and every value. For example, women, ethnic minorities, gays or the disabled may be a marginalized subgroup within a community. Sexism and racism are wrong. They are also divisive, and impede action for positive social change, and in fact are frequently the targets for organizing. But to try to deal with them head-on within the community - without first establishing personal credibility or an understanding of their experience - is an approach that gains the organizer a "preachy" reputation. When the organizer has gained credibility, it may be important to help community members question some of their attitudes and practices.

Contacts should be broad. This is not necessarily easy. When we first make contact with the community we may find that we are dealing with a narrow range of people. Usually, the people privileged by their race, gender, ability, or education levels are the ones who have the higher profiles. However, try not to stay with an "elite". Find out who has power and credibility; and who can mobilize others, and who does not, and why. There has been more than one organizer who became attached to an initially attractive, or noisy, group only to find out later that the members were only narrowly representative. Also, when a citizens' group is seeking funds for a project, or confronting a bureaucrat or politician, the question will invariably be asked: "Just whom do you represent? How broad is your support?" Speeter (1978: 33) offers the following list for types of people to look for:

- those interested in community change;
- those who will work to get others involved (door knock, phone calls, etc.);
- youth leaders;
- elderly leaders;
- leaders of groups or organizations;
- people who can speak in front of large crowds;

We would add:

- leadership among women or minorities;
- not only existing leadership, but leadership potential in the community;
- those with good listening skills;
- those interested in learning;
- those who can work cooperatively with others.

A few other things to look for when entering and engaging:

- potential for economic benefits - unused or underutilized resources;
- issues that people are likely to coalesce around (either positive or negative);
- functioning groups or organizations (formal or informal);
- things and processes that show ability - though people may not always be aware of that ability;
- signs of hope - little things that people have accomplished themselves;
- human resources - skills and energy, or connections to power outside the community;
- economic/philanthropic - business/entrepreneurship, etc.;
- people working to help each other.

All of this should be done carefully, however. It is important to remember that, simply because something works well in one setting, this does not mean that it will work well in others. While we must always be prepared to be sensitive to local conditions, it is particularly important in this beginning phase.

> **Example:** A worker was hired by a teachers' union to do some organizing with parents concerned about education issues in the county of Peel in Ontario. The first meeting he organized with these groups went extremely well - the participants were able to identify concerns, issues (in this case, concerns about the quality of resources in local schools) and tasks. They immediately started work, and began suggesting other areas where meetings should be organized. Unfortunately, the next couple of meetings were not as successful - people came out but showed a lot of hesitancy in getting to specific issues, and reluctance to get involved in action. After some reflection, the worker realized that the success of the first meeting was linked to specific local conditions. Many of the parents had known each other from various community and school events. One

of the teachers involved had actually known the organizer from a project he had been involved in several years earlier. Here there was a bedrock of familiarity and trust. In the other groups, these conditions did not exist - the people were new to each other and to the organizer. It was not that parents were less concerned - indeed, there were good turnouts - but the pace of getting people involved had to be slower so they had time to get a sense of each other and the organizer. The organizer needed to attend to initial, local conditions.

Once the organizer feels he has contact with reasonably representative and credible people, the interest of the funding institution (in providing a community organizer) can and must be shared publicly. Sometimes, however, funders or sponsors are not aware of the complexity of community work.

Example: A worker was hired by a women's centre to do some organizing around the needs of immigrant seniors (predominantly women). The centre had gotten a sense, through its drop-in and settlement services, that elderly folks were feeling quite isolated and lonely. The response of the administration was to develop an undertaking that would be aimed at linking people with resources - such as, public health and recreation. It was thought that this would be a fairly simple project. The worker, however, quickly found that she was confronted by a complex grouping of eight cultural communities. Initially it was thought that she would go in and ask some nice clear questions about needs and resources. What she found was that she would need to take time to get a sense of the cultural mores, where people lived, how the various groups received information, and what relationships existed among the groups. She had to do some education with the centre director.

This does not mean that the organizer has been secretive about this up until now; nor does it mean that he must now call a meeting, or make some sort of public announcement. He may simply start making it more clear to people "why" he is there," what" the mandate is from the sponsor, and "how" people can begin to get together.

Reflection

Entering and beginning to connect meaningfully with people is a crucial element in the organizing process. It can also be one of the most confusing times in the project - the organizer doesn't usually know many of the people, and the community may be quite diverse and dispersed. Things may seem (and probably are) quite complex. This is a bad news/good news situation. Most of us like a little control in our work; but this is a very fluid time, with new people and perspectives coming at us all the time. The good news is that we are capable of recognizing this, and of reflecting on the fact that it is not we who are causing the complexity. We have no responsibility for knowing it all, let alone understanding it - this is the beginning of analysis. There is strength in seeing ourselves as being at the beginning of a journey, one in which we will learn, and in which we shall become more deeply involved. At this point we are looking for people who wish to travel with us, and for things that will assist us along the road.

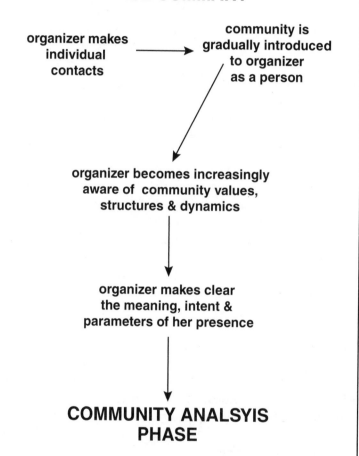

CONTACT & ENGAGEMENT PHASE SUMMARY

organizer makes individual contacts → community is gradually introduced to organizer as a person

organizer becomes increasingly aware of community values, structures & dynamics

organizer makes clear the meaning, intent & parameters of her presence

COMMUNITY ANALSYIS PHASE

Chapter

6

COMMUNITY ANALYSIS

Critical investigation helps people to look at social problems in the light of what they wish to achieve as self-reliant and self-determining social beings.
—Susan McGrath (Teacher and Activist)

It is important as an organizer begins acting in the community, that she attend to the notion that the community is an organism. That is, it is complex (has parts that are interrelated), and is in flux (the parts are moving). It is important that community members understand this as well. Remember that social learning is a key objective of community development. Freire (1970: 71) says that it is crucial that the people "come to see the world not as a static reality, but as reality in process, in transformation". An important role for the organizer, at this stage, is facilitator of learning.

In some respects, community analysis is a continuation of the contact and engagement phase. The organizer is becoming more visible, not as a leader, but as someone who **cares** about the people and the issues, and who appears **confident** that the citizens can work together and produce something of good quality. Members are forming clearer conceptions of her. The important difference is that while previously the organizer was getting information primarily for her own use, this phase involves information gathering and analysis for the community's self development. While in the entry phase, the organizer was the primary investigator. In the community analysis phase, community people must begin to question, and gain an understanding of, their own community. The objective of community sense comes into play here.

They must begin to get a sense of themselves as a distinct group with particular problems and strengths. (Speeter, 1978) While there are standard types of information that need to be gathered, questions generated **within and by the members** will also be very important.

At this point we can make some assumptions:

- the organizer has spent some time "in" the community;
- she has some notions about the values and the people in the community;
- she has made a firm link with a group of people, probably small, and her existence is known by a reasonably wide range of community members;
- the small core group may be formal or informal, but the members have some credibility, and can likely wield some clout within the community;
- if the community already has a leadership structure in place, the worker has a sense of others with leadership potential;
- she is beginning to have some conception of the problems faced by the community;
- she has some awareness of the diverse interest or reference groups in the community.

At this point it is tempting to launch directly into action to solve some obvious and serious problem. **Be careful!** There are some major pitfalls to this approach. For example, the base of support or action is small and needs to be broadened. Action (even on a most important issue) without **consensus** and a **broad base of support** tends to be short lived, frustrating, and leads to burnout. It can be divisive as well.

> **Example:** A new worker in an inner city neighborhood knew that an obvious problem there was high unemployment. When he was approached by a small group of people to help them organize a local economic development project it seemed to make sense. Difficulties quickly arose however, when some other groups in the area raised questions as to whether the project would primarily benefit just that particular group, but

not help anyone else. As the issue became more public, serious opposition arose, and community divisions (already existing) became worse. It wasn't that the original idea was a bad
one - it had simply moved too quickly. The project never got
off the ground, and the worker had to spend a lot of time mending fences.

There may well be other issues that are seen as more important, or at
least linked to the ones that first appear. There is not likely any
community consensus at this point. **Action without a community
consensus leads to division and failure.**

It is necessary to develop a strategy to avoid these pitfalls. The strategy
must include:

- **clear problem definitions** – the what? where? when? who? how?
  and why? must become clearly understood so that appropriate
  strategies and tactics can be developed (Stinson, 1979);
- a solid **community consensus** around those problem definitions
  (Stinson, 1979);
- an understanding within the community of itself – a **community
  image;**
- an **organizational base** from which to deal with the problems.
  This involves the   development of-
  - *Participation* – committed, animated people prepared to work
    on specific concerns;
  - *Leadership* – confident, sensitive people with vision prepared
    to work and involve others;
  - *Coherence* – focused and relevant analysis plus effective use
    of human resources.

What we are going to talk about here, as one means of meeting these
objectives, is the mounting of a community research project - one that
might take eight months to a year to complete. The kind of research
suggested here is linked to a variety of structural traditions; the main
ones being feminist and participatory action research.[1] Reinharz (1992,
p.175) describes feminist research as being inherently linked to action.
The purpose of feminist research must be to create new relationships,

better laws, and improved institutions. Participatory action research focuses on the following principles: "..the people studied make decisions about the study format and data analysis,...the research ...adopts an approach of openness, reciprocity, mutual disclosure, and shared risk" (Reinharz 1992, p.181). So essentially we are talking about a kind of research that is political, and geared toward popular control and social transformation.

Two key ingredients are invariably missing from disorganized communities: information and analysis. Solid information is an important underpinning for a community to analyze itself and its situation. Information which **people** can **share** is necessary to enable **them** to see their **commonalities,** and to become **involved** in a process of **consensus, action** and **change. Analysis** is a process of reflection, during which time members talk to one another in a manner that enables them to learn about their situation and themselves, and to appreciate their own understanding and analysis of their experience. (See Figure 6-1: Action/Reflection Spiral).

To facilitate community involvement (remember the citizen involvement objective), a participatory action research methodology is most appropriate. People often have a deep-seated distrust of any kind of research, and/or of getting together with others. This is legitimate, in that it is often a reflection of their experience. People may say: "Why bother? Nobody really cares anyway."; "It won't work, we tried it before."; or "This will only benefit those in power!". It is an issue that needs to be understood and managed. Participatory action research is a process that needs to be experienced if people are to develop confidence in themselves, or faith in the procedure. Part of the process is learning about, and understanding, their community history; and how such a history may affect how people see themselves and their environment. This means that the people of the community should be deeply involved, not only in giving information and hearing about results, but also in developing the questions to be asked, and in doing much of the questioning themselves. They must be in charge. Action research has another important aspect which is: **question should stimulate question**. This **analytical process** should, in effect, never end. Through it the community begins to know and feel itself, to develop a sense of community, and to engage in some social learning. It may be that there is little or no community identity feeling, prior to this process. Often this is true. Ideally, the people raise their consciousness of themselves as a collective, and begin to specify objectives in relation to a particular situation or problem.

As well as being useful for a community that is developing its self-concept and raising important issues, participatory action research can begin to highlight people with leadership potential – persons who show particular interest, creativity, or charisma with respect to the issues that arise. Finally, an action research effort can help to de-mystify research, and assist members to develop their own research skills.

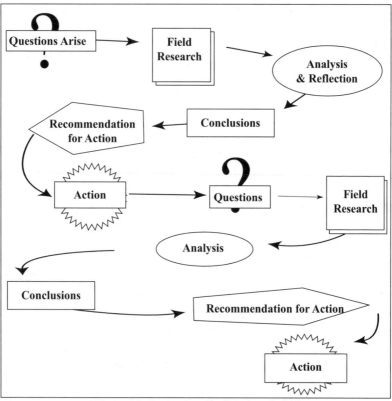

Figure 1-6: Action Reflection Spiral

Adapted from *Do it Yourself Social Research* (1984) by Yoland Wadsworth, Victorian Council of Social Services, Melbourne: Allen & Unwin

An Open-Ended Process

It is important to remember that this whole analytical process will likely continue for some time, somewhat loose and unstructured. It can lead, in the short run, to blind alleys. It can also drive us crazy if we expect results quickly. Hang in, and try to move with the grain of the community as it raises and drops and raises its issues **at its pace**, and as new people become involved, and leadership develops and broadens.

> **Example:** The action group "Single Mothers Against Poverty", in Hamilton, used the organizing assistance of students and a faculty member of McMaster University School of Social Work to do an action research project. This group of individual single mothers on Family Benefits Assistance grew from a nucleus of five people to over twenty members. They were able to produce two research reports dealing with the experience of single parenthood and poverty. For over five years they were a significant organization on the Hamilton scene, and were instrumental in affecting changes in local welfare administration concerning single mothers. The initial organizing strategy was that of Participatory Action Research, which helped them identify issues, and helped motivate these single mothers to take action.

Participatory Action Research[2]

> *We create knowledge so that we can better understand the meaning of our own experience and identity, and the complexity of the society in which we live. It is a process of understanding who we are, and determining how we want to be. Knowledge should help us to understand our current experience and to develop alternative ways of living that respond to the issues identified.*
>
> —*Susan McGrath (Teacher and Activist)*

Step 1

A group of representative community members (people whom the organizer, and trusted community members, perceive as having potential to work together and provide broader leadership) are invited to meet to discuss things they think they know about their community and want confirmed, as well as questions they have about their community to which they want answers. In a community that is relatively organized, the worker may have to ask the formal leaders to invite the people. This provides a legitimacy for the endeavor, though there may be a problem of the group being less representative than one would like. This issue would have to be raised as the idea is presented to the community leaders. At this point, the group has at best an unclear and diffuse concept of what the important issues are, and how they are generally viewed. They may have some ideas, but little precise data to either back up or contradict their thoughts or ideas. There will likely be a good deal of disagreement, or contradiction, or at least a wide range of ideas about the community. (This is true even within an established group). This situation is not a weakness, but is actually a strength. (Freire, 1970: 104). During this stage the organizer must assist the group to use this diversity of concept to get all the possible aspects of the community. In fact the community worker will want to model a stance of acceptance of diversity. The first task of this step, then, is to help the group to brainstorm around what elements make up the community – physical, social, psychological, political, etc..

During this process we need to be attentive to those people not oriented to print media (rural peasants or new immigrants, etc.). Some organizers have done some interesting and very useful work using popular education techniques, drawings, maps, cartoons, etc. (Hope & Timmel, 1984; Barndt & Freire, 1989; Lee & Balkwill, 1996)

Community group comes together to discuss housing issues in Mississauga.

Step II

The second task is to construct some sort of survey instrument out of the brainstorming that will enable the group to begin to query the community. The organizer will want to make sure that particular standard areas and methods are covered. A non-exclusive list of important areas is offered, but first it is important to remember that different groups have different ways of understanding, valuing, and sharing knowledge. The format for collecting information from members should be sensitive to specific community ways and needs. Several workers have shared stories of how questionnaires had sometimes proven to be an inappropriate means of gathering information in some groups. In particular, these workers referred to their work with homeless people, and with Native Peoples. In both situations it was found that knowledge was shared as "stories", not as responses to specific questions. And while many of these stories may have initially appeared to be irrelevant, or not directly connected to the issues being addressed, with careful listening one finds them to be dense with information - especially those issues of importance to community members.

Economic
- Income range of the population;
- Occupation inventory and the number of members involved in each type. Among other things, information of this type might highlight particular skills existing in the community.

Demographic
- Age ranges;
- Family size and make-up (e.g., the number of single parent families or the number of female-led families, etc.);
  Gender ratio;
- Range of people with disabilities and their types.

Education
- Levels,
- Types: technical, professional, on the job training and workshops, life experience.

Religion or Spirituality
- Formal,
- Informal.

Geographic
- Where members live: social classes, age groups, racial groups, ethnic groups, or disabled people;
- Important geographical features ;
- The physical placement of important institutions or services (e.g., churches, day care centres, businesses and shopping). It can be fun and instructive to have people draw a large organizational map of all the institutions that impact in/on the community (Lee& Balkwill, 1996). This exercise can get people talking about how they feel about the organizations. This information is just as valuable as the locations and sizes of agencies.

Power Structure
- What constitutes power – money, information, numbers and status – within this   community, particularly in relation to attacking possible community difficulties. A force field analysis exercise can be useful here.
- Splits and alignments. Who lines up with whom, or against whom, on what specific issues? The construction and use of a sociogram or force field analysis can be useful (Lee and Balkwill, 1996). As with organizational mapping, a good conversation and a sense of feeling will likely emerge here.

Problem Definitions
- How do people see the problems?
- Do they see any as interrelated? For example, "There is a lot of apathy around here [first problem] because a few people run everything [second problem]".
- To what extent do they feel personally affected by the problems?
- How deep or sophisticated are the analyses? Are they connecting local or specific problems to structural issues, like unemployment or some form of discrimination?

Vision or Visions for the Future
- What are the ideas (hopes and dreams) of what the community should look like in the future or how it should operate?
- Is there a reasonable amount of consensus, or are there competing visions that will need to be negotiated?

Emotional Tenor
- How is the community or various parts of the community feeling? Are there feelings of:
  - contentment?
  - anger?
  - hope or despair? This will in part depend on the extent to which people have a positive vision for themselves.
  - apathy, i.e., a sense that things can be done but the effort isn't worth it? Again this might be linked to vision.
  - energy for action?

Resources
- Physical - eg. community centre,
- Education, social and health services, churches, etc..

Other Considerations

The way these questions are asked, the amount of stress placed on the various areas, and the language used must be that of the community. Watch out for technical terms – e.g., validity and reliability – which we may (or may not) well understand, but which may not be familiar to the people. Also, some subcultures have particular ways of expressing themselves – everything from slang to the use of stories and concrete examples. This must be considered as the instrument is constructed. Remember there are two objectives to building such a survey: first, to come up with an instrument that will provide clear and honest responses; second, to begin to involve people in their own process of analyzing – i.e., in "understanding" – their own community. It is crucial then to make the survey-building process public (Warren, 1977) and invitational. This can be done by getting the core group to:

- Ask members at large to suggest questions. People on the survey committee should approach friends and acquaintances and invite them to think about giving them questions they would like to see added.
- Check out various aspects of their developing survey instrument and process with others in the community – the language, timing, etc.
- Invite people who become interested by the questioning activity to join the core group.
- Invite people to volunteer for short periods of time to do small tasks that they might be interested in doing, like delivering and picking up questionnaires.

What you are attempting to facilitate is not only a generalized knowledge and involvement, but the creation among all community members of a real stake in having the process come off as successfully as possible (Warren, 1977). This survey instrument, to be an accurate and valuable document for the community, must in every sense belong to it, and not just to the original survey committee.

It is one thing to develop a questionnaire or interview schedule. It is another thing to have it completed successfully; that is, have a high degree of returns and have good information to analyze.

We are probably going to be asking personal information or at least information that people perceive as personal. It is important that the group from the very first moment stress that all responses are completely confidential. As well, groups of people who are disadvantaged are often justly suspicious of people who ask them to fill in forms or ask them questions. Thus, it is worthwhile to take some pains not only to treat the information with great care, but to **show** that you do so as well. Intra-community trust is one of the things your group, and you as an organizer are trying to facilitate, so everything that relates to that dynamic is important.

A participant in a popular education exercise presents her group's analysis.

Step III

An interim report will have to be made to the community in some way – a couple of "fact sheets" may be all that is necessary. As well, a community meeting should be organized to present the report. (More on meetings in the next chapter). The completion of the survey, and the analysis and sharing of the results, will provide the community with a much clearer image of itself. Some old ideas will have been confirmed, others will have been shown to be untrue or exaggerated, and finally information about the community that no one expected to find will have invariably been uncovered. Most important, however, is that the image that develops at this point will be commonly held and based on facts. This allows the members to talk about their community, using the same information.

Questionnaire or Interview Schedule

1. A questionnaire is sent out or delivered to community members. There is minimal or no personal contact. In a questionnaire we are not attempting to get a great deal of, or very sophisticated information.

2. On the other hand, with an interview schedule we are getting people to sit down with each other, probably because the information desired is a little complex and participants may need some help or encouragement in giving all the information required.

3. Some general rules to use when trying to decide which is best for our group are as follows:

    •   The larger the population we need to question, the more likely we will have to use a questionnaire because of the difficulty in getting personally to everyone.
    •   The more complex the information that we want, the more likely we will want to use an interview format. This will allow the volunteers to help people interpret the questions and encourage them to be complete in their answers.
    •   Obviously, with an interview schedule we are going to have to have a large number of volunteers to contact and to sit down with people. These volunteers will have to be trained – either by the organizer or by other members of the survey team – in how the questions are to be asked and how to answer any questions that participants may have.
    •   Be sure that we are clear on what kind of instrument we are constructing – interview schedule or questionnaire. Depending on the people involved and the kind of information that we are trying to get, you will want to do one or the other. In one Native community a group of people developed a very interesting interview schedule. They hoped that, in the process of the person to person contact, some community building could go on. Unfortunately, their system of training interviewers was not very rigorous, and many of the people who volunteered lacked confidence. They simply handed out the interview schedules to people and asked them to fill them out, like a questionnaire. Not surprisingly, much of the information gathered was superficial or not very clear. The exercise had been designed as an interactive one, and failed as a simple questionnaire.

Step IV

The fourth step is, ideally, a second round of questioning. As presented here, it is in the form of an individual questionnaire. It is possible to combine the interim report meeting and the questioning session. In this case we would want to use a small group format and choose and train facilitators. The advantage of this is that the process is quicker. The disadvantage is that we may not get to nearly as many people.

As we have discussed before, a community is a living thing and is in constant motion. The first survey is probably going to miss things; some information that was turned up may be confusing to the members; or some things may have changed. Thus, a second round of questioning can be very useful. This does not mean that, if some extremely clear issues have emerged in the first round, no action should be planned.[3] In fact, it is these very issues that should form a major focus for the second round of questioning.

Another aspect of this step is that it should be more personal or immediate than the first one. There should be more interaction between those seeking the information, and those giving it. Thus an interview, as opposed to a questionnaire format, should be used. This can be done partly because we are now working on the highlights raised by the first round, and there will be a much shorter schedule of questions. This more personal approach is necessitated by the fact that:

1. We are going after more subtle types of information now – feelings, detailed opinion and attitudes, etc.

2. We want to make the process absolutely as open as possible – it is important to capture every nuance; not only do you need answers to questions, but a sense of how people felt about the questions and answers.

3. Organizing is a human endeavour - making this an interview format stresses the human, face-to-face nature of what we are doing.

4.   We are really trying to flesh out concrete action targets now, trying to instill a sense of immediacy (even crisis if there is one) so that people will be motivated to get involved to take action. This step cannot be executed at long range. Only people interacting with each other can achieve this.

The process of constructing the interview guide, or popular education exercise, or whatever kind of process the group decides upon, is identical to that used to come up with the first survey. It will obviously take less time the second time around, though just as much effort.

> **Note:** Be prepared. The people may want to construct another questionnaire or interview guide. They've just come through a successful experience with questionnaires or interviews. They feel that they have become good at it. It is natural for all of us to want to do the things that we are good at; nevertheless, they must be helped to further develop their abilities, and to get on with taking action on, and using, the knowledge they have developed.

The actual format might look something like this:

1.   A limited number of statements (no more than 6) are made based on data from the first survey. The respondents have all seen the "interim report" so that statements aren't new. (For example X per cent of people feel that there is a big problem with the absentee landlord; or Y per cent of the population are children between 6 and 10 years of age).

2.   The interviewer elicits opinions and feelings about the statements. For example:
    •   Is the respondent surprised by them? Why or why not?
    •   Is she happy or angry? Why or why not?

3.   If the respondent appears really interested in one or more of the issues, the interviewer asks her if she would be interested in:
    •   Receiving more information?
    •   Finding out how other members feel about the issue?

- Coming to a meeting with other members, if one were to take place?

Note: Remember our strategy objectives from page 97.
1. Problem definition
2. Consensus
3. Community Image
4. Building a community organization
   - Participation
   - Leadership

This part of the strategy is focused on getting things off the ground and on the way to achieving solutions to those identified problems. Thus, the people recruited to do the interviewing are taking on a special responsibility and will probably need some group meetings to provide them with:

1. Training – from the organizer and/or each other;
2. Encouragement – from the organizer;
3. Group Support – from each other.

All three are necessary because most people are not used to doing this kind of thing and need to have some reassurance. In effect, what we are hoping for is that the citizens of the community will begin to organize themselves. They are going to need help from their organizer, but the community should really be in control.

Step V

The point of all this activity is to assist the community to get a solid sense of the issues that its members feel they should, and can, work on. Thus it is important to disseminate analysis throughout the community. This can be done by compiling a final report and getting it out either through a series of meetings, or mailings, or drop offs. Even people who were not involved in the other processes might find themselves interested if they can identify with any of the issues and recommendations for action in our report.

Reflection

> **Example:** A small inner city neighbourhood association had
> been dormant for some time and the community had been ex-
> periencing a number of problems - vandalism, booze cans, poor
> city services to the area, etc. Five local women along with a
> volunteer organizer had been trying to get people together for
> about a year, without much success. Finally they did a small
> action research project. They talked to people about what they
> were finding, and were able to identify some key issues for
> residents and some ideas around strategy. They finally called a
> meeting to check the interest. To their delight they got a large
> turnout of local residents who responded strongly to the range
> of issues, and the strategies that had been identified to the small
> group of activists.

The example shows clearly that people need some leadership, and
clearly focused information that is relevant to their experience, before
they come to feel that they want to become involved in a community
change process. The community analysis phase is a crucial step in the
development of community capacity. We are addressing the issue of
knowledge creation, or social learning. Also, in the identification and
involvement of new leaders, and the identification of action targets,
"organization development" is being addressed.

Learning is one of the central objectives undertaken with a popular
education approach. It contributes to other objectives - such as, sense
of community and participation. Indeed social learning should become
a habit, and the action/reflection process can contribute to the long
term development of the community.

Endnotes

[1]   There are a number of good books and monographs on research for people's organizations: *Community Research as Empowerment* by Ristock and Penell; *Participatory Action Research* by Fals-Borda and Rahman (1991); *Research for Change* by J. Barnesley and D Ellis (1992). Another is Australian activist Yoland Wadsworth's *Do It Yourself Social Research* (1984).

[2]   The model suggested here was field tested in housing co-operatives by Mike Balkwill, and in anti-poverty work with women by Sharon MacQueen. It is a comprehensive one aimed at developing a good deal of information, and at building a strong organized informed citizen group. It requires considerable time. Circumstances may dictate an alternative or scaled down approach. That's ok. However, keep in mind that this is first and foremost a community and organization building tool. As long as we are clear on the implications of what we do, the benefits will turn out to be largely what we expected.

[3]   In some ways this step can belong to the chapter on Action because it is very much action-oriented. It is presented here, however, for reasons of simplicity and coherence.

COMMUNITY ANALYSIS
PHASE SUMMARY

organizer arranges for
small group of community
people to meet to share
ideas & questions about
their community

organizer facilitates ideas
& questions by sharing
them with other community
members - others invited
to join group

survey instrument is constructed
& timetable for its distribution
developed

survey is administered to community
- whole or representative sample

information is collected
& analyzed by the group

report is written &
distributed throughout
the community

highlights of surveys
developed into an action
oriented system

second survey is
administered in a
personal manner

action targets
clarified &
solidified

interested individuals
& groups are identified
and recruited

ORGANIZATION DEVELOPMENT
PHASE

7

ORGANIZATION DEVELOPMENT

Our success with social change depends on our ability to implement our visions within our own organizations, even as we work toward them in the outside world.
—Duane Dale and Nancy Mitiguy (1978)

The title "Organization Development" is used because it is in this part of the process that specific issues begin to appear publicly as targets for action[1]. As noted previously, we can only act if we are organized – that is, if we have structures and processes to marshal community resources over time. The major organizing effort must now go into building structures and strategies that can tackle the targets. Activity should become less diffuse and more concentrated on particular issues and associated tasks. Also, the project should be quite well on the way to being the "community's project" as opposed to the "X Agency Community Project". This means that if leaders were not visible when the organizer began, they should be emerging sufficiently to take on major organizational responsibilities. If leadership was in place prior to entry, it should now look broader and increasingly more skillful and thus the organization should be "more developed."

Meetings

It is important that the community reinforce the habit of consulting itself regarding its objectives and the strategies for reaching them - this is part of "citizenship". It also builds an organization that can tackle serious problems that affect its members. It is essential that this organization be an open, democratic people's organization (Alinsky, 1970). Meetings are a major tactic for informing, involving and mobilizing citizens.

After an action research process, the problems have become reasonably well perceived and understood by a majority of members. The community is now ready for a variety of meetings – general community, task groups, committees, etc.

First meetings are particularly important to get things well off the ground. Particularly at the beginning of an organization's life, some "pre-meeting" meetings may have to be held. These should include the formal leaders and other key actors; and might focus on important individual positions, internal disagreements, building confidence and enthusiasm; and agreeing on general, but flexible, directions for the first general meeting.

This first meeting is a model of how well the people can bring something off. It is not necessary (or possible) to have all the answers right away. It is necessary for the leadership to be prepared to lead the people in the direction they see as most likely to provide answers. At the same time, leaders must be prepared to:

- listen to the membership;
- offer what suggestions they have;
- accept criticism and the shaping of their suggestions or the building of new ones.

Community group meeting to discuss the potential for a housing advocacy organization.

This is no place for an ego trip (especially the organizer's), though it is reasonable and important to feel good for any job well done, and to be recognized for it.

It is very important that the people leave the meeting knowing that something is going to be done, and that specific members have volunteered to take on the tasks. This sets some reasonable expectations, and suggests that this organization is for action, not just talk. This is an early period and people are new to this, so the organizer must be prepared to help this along.

> **Example**: An organizer in a downtown Toronto neighborhood was present as the group was just coming to the end of its first meeting. The two women co-chairs had done a great job of setting the agenda, encouraging constructive discussion, and helping people identify some important issues. There was a good feeling in the room. At this point he noticed that both the

women looked a little distressed and seemed a *bit lost.* *He* also noticed that no committees had been struck to take on the issues. So he raised his hand for permission to speak. He suggested the meeting strike about five committees to cover the issues and take some initial action. Almost immediately people started volunteering, and a little later the meeting ended on an upbeat note. During a "post meeting" meeting with the co-chairs, the two women thanked him for his timely intervention; they had gotten temporarily lost in all the information that had come out. They then reflected on all the good things they and the members had accomplished that evening.

1. Major Objectives of a First Meeting

a)   To present a clear picture of the problems as analyzed up to this moment.

b)   To take a general issue and turn it into a specific action target.

c)   To serve notice to the community and others that some members of the community are prepared to work to solve a particular configuration of problems and issues.

d)   To begin to recruit workers for the problem-solving efforts.

e)   To offer tentative or beginning strategies – not a grand design – for people working together on the common effort.

f)   To mobilize volunteer effort.

2. Raising Issues

a)   Any issue that is chosen early in this phase should be clearly "do-able" or winnable. Remember, a community that needs a community organizer may not have a great deal of confidence. A quick loss could destroy the credibility of the leadership and organizer; the organizing effort could easily get set back.

b) It should be possible to link sub-issues to the major one - e.g., "Not only is there a drug problem in our neighbourhood, but the police are slow to react to a call from residents. Have you noticed that we seem to get inferior municipal services here?"

c) The leaders, or most of them, should be associated with the issue (i.e., have a stake in the problem).

3. Post-Meetings

Equally as important as a "pre-meeting" is a "post-meeting". The meeting itself has hopefully produced some desirable results – issues clarified; participation increased and broadened; some objectives outlined; priorities set. Now it's important to have those involved (including new activists who have emerged at the meeting) take a look at what has gone on. Alinsky suggests that an organizer must assist the citizens to learn through their experience. This is a crucial technique that the organizer must always use – the processing of every major event can not only assist people to learn for future action, but can often bring out creative strategy for immediate use.

What is the organizer's stance during these three events - pre-, during- and post-meeting?

a) She must be analytical – never presuming to have all the answers, and always open to ideas. A model for the people.

b) She must constantly believe (and live out that belief) that the people will come to the right decisions – perhaps not right away, or maybe not without conflict or assistance, but eventually.

4. Ensuring the Best Possible Attendance

It is common to hear experienced, hard working volunteer members complaining about apathy demonstrated by other members of the community. Poor attendance at meetings is one of the major concerns and frustrations one hears in community organizing. Factually this is true. It is indeed a real problem which often gets in the way of community problem-solving. However, when considering this problem, it is important to keep in mind some other facts such as:

a) Community members are also family members, and;

b) They are also workers (outside and inside the home). People have conflicting demands on their time. For all but the most dedicated, community responsibilities are going to rank number three on any three item list. This does not mean that it is hopeless to expect people to come to meetings. It is a matter of appreciating the fact of competing and sometimes unpredictable demands in an individual's personal and work life. It means helping the leadership do a little organizing in the light of those demands.

Note: Unorganized or disorganized communities are not generally used to meetings (Speeter, 1978). The structure and formality may be new for many people, somewhat outside of their experience. Thus, try to make sure that the social needs as well as the business needs of the community group are attended to, e.g., perhaps coffee, and donuts or small talk time. Also, different cultural groups conduct meetings in various ways. We need to be sensitive to differences and be prepared to learn from them as well as manage them.

c) Give people as much notice as possible. This is especially important for first or irregular meetings.

d) Put it in writing. Leaflets and posters are helpful. Sometimes a local community newspaper will do inexpensive advertisements.
   - Remember that communities are made up of sub-groups. Have the range of languages covered.

Example: A Hamilton organizer was working in a project with three major language groups: Filipino, Vietnamese and English. He had to make sure to get quality translations for all leaflets and handouts.

e)   Remind them. A visit, phone call and/or leaflet blitz within twenty-four hours of the event is a good idea. Develop telephone or visiting trees. The community worker may be part of this, but should not do it all.

f)   It may be important for the organizer and leadership to do some visiting, encouraging individuals to talk-up the issue and the event, letting people know how important it is. Individuals may need to know in a direct personal way that their involvement will be valued. There are other payoffs in doing this activity:
      • It provides a firmer idea of who is, and who is not, coming;
      • It lessens likelihood of the leadership experiencing last minute disappointment;
      • It provides a sense of how the issue or issues are shaping up.

5.   Preparation for Meetings

Meetings are rarely for information sharing only. Almost always there is some kind of decision to be made. Thus, the participants in the meeting need to have sufficient information so they can make realistic decisions.

•   *Information: What kind?* Start with ourselves and put us into a participant's shoes. With that perspective, value our own judgement and encourage the groups we are working with to do the same. Chances are if we want to know something, others will too.

•   *Information: Where is it or who has it?* In effect, information (which is an important power element, remember) may be everywhere. The problem is that it has not been brought together. That is one of the reasons we're building an organization and having the meeting - to bring people and information together and to engage in a decision-making process so that some problem can be solved.

When we are thinking of where to obtain information, be creative. Information is not only facts – it is perspective, attitude, opinion; even rumour is sometimes important. Thus we have to look everywhere, in and outside the community. For example, if we are working with a number of tenants to organize a meeting to do something about a neglectful landlord, a broad array of information will be helpful:

- relevant legislation and regulations – found at municipal or provincial offices;
- rent scales – may be found inside or outside;
- the experiences of the tenants with the landlord;
- experiences that other communities have had with other landlords;
- their own experience with each other.

> **Example**: The Hamilton worker mentioned earlier found that there was little contact but lots of negative stereotyping and distrust among the three language/culture groups in his project. This had serious implications for how meetings could be organized and how he approached each group.

It is rather like doing the community survey again – ideally everyone needs to be contacted – only the issue is much more focused and imminent. Try to make a point of contacting people in person (community organizing involves a lot of leg work). Continuous and exclusive use of "paper talk" (such as flyers and posters) can eventually be "off-putting". Knock on doors or at least phone. Tell them why you want their data or opinion or experience – people sometimes tend to downgrade the importance of their own ideas because they are not clearly formed. Sometimes they need time and encouragement. Even if a person does not have much to say now, she will likely appreciate being asked and this can pay dividends.

- It may spark or rekindle interest in the issue. Thus, they may make it a priority to get to the meeting.

- When another issue comes up that "grabs" them, they may then see the group as interested and caring and bring it to the organizer.

Finally, *what do we do with information?* It is one thing to get data; it is another thing to make the best use of it. Sometimes it is sufficient to have information ready for use at a meeting. At other times it is important to get some clear and concise written material out to participants prior to the meeting. (Again, language may be an issue).

Getting it out beforehand has a number of payoffs:

*   It increases familiarity with the issues and thus the meetings can get into "high gear" sooner;

*   It may clarify or increase the participant's sense of purpose;

*   It may give some participants a chance to think over, alter, or clarify their position;

*   It gives participants a chance to spot and question incorrect data prior to the meeting;

*   It gives people a chance to lose it or forget it – so be sure to have extra copies if possible.

    Note: Help the group to be as clear and concise as possible to avoid information overload.

6. People Preparation

As we said before, at the beginning of an organization's life the participants may be unfamiliar with meetings, and may need some assistance in getting themselves set for them.

*   Be sure people have a clear perception of why it is that they are getting together.

*   Be sure the group has arranged for a discussion leader or chairperson. This person should be identified prior to the meeting. The person may need to get psyched up (or calmed down) or she might want to seek you out for support.

Example: The Single Mothers Against Poverty group in Hamilton used a rotating "chair" as they began. The members were very inexperienced, and the organizer used to spend a couple of hours with each person before each meeting. It didn't totally alleviate anxiety, but it was reduced when the women felt that they had some"training" and were not completely on their own.

There will likely be a need for a secretary - someone to record what happens and what decisions are made. (Watch out for inadvertent sex role stereotyping.)

Note: One of the attributes a group is looking for here is assertiveness. The person chosen to do the recording must be able to say to the meeting "Can I have that again?" "Can you say that a bit more clearly?"

Example: A student organizer, in a housing co-op, recruited a woman to take the minutes of a meeting. He didn't check with her beforehand as to whether she had any experience in recording minutes – it's not an easy job. When the woman circulated the minutes prior to the next meeting they were pretty well unintelligible. The worker had to approach her and help her do some new ones in a hurry. Naturally her feelings were hurt, and other committee members were irritated at being represented so poorly. The worker had to do a good deal of work to get things straight and smooth ruffled feathers. He realized that if he had talked to and assisted the woman in the first place, he would have saved a lot of work and fuss.

It is important that meetings don't get dominated by a small group. For example, we know that generally women have been socialized to be less assertive than men (Gallagher, 1977); that people with higher education tend to be more vocal than those with less (Repo, 1977); and that some immigrant groups will have difficulty with English. If our group is going to be truly democratic it is going to have to break through these obstacles and facilitate broader involvement.

- Get to the more timid folks and let them know their ideas and opinions are important.

- Remind the leadership that some members need patience and perhaps help in clarifying their presentations.

- Suggest to the more articulate and vociferous participants (diplomatically of course) that they restrain their own participation somewhat so that the more timid voices can be heard.

- A special caucus might be organized to give groups, like women or immigrants, a chance to share and think things through before a more general meeting.

Example: The Hamilton organizer mentioned above had to organize three meetings for the three different groups to get at some of the stereotyping and distrust. These small meetings were useful in helping people articulate issues that were explicit to them. For example, one of the groups tended to focus on cars and vandalism, while another group had practically no drivers among them and was more concerned about safety issues. Eventually the two issues had to be seen as part of the same dynamic.

Note: One way of structuring a positive environment is to suggest that the group develop its own "Safety Rules" (Lee & Balkwill, 1996). Here members develop a list of rules for their own conduct at meetings such as: "no laughing at naive questions", or "no shouting down a person with whom you don't agree."   Different groups will have different lists depending on their own experience. It is empowering to have influence over the process you are going to have to use.

7. Site Preparation: Instrumental Considerations

The real job of an organizer is first, to get to the hall early, make sure the doors are open, the lights turned on, the coffee's ready and that there are enough chairs for everyone. The second thing is to stay behind and make sure the room is cleaned up, the chairs are put away, the lights are turned out and the doors are locked.

—Worker for the Company of Young Canadians

There is great wisdom in the above observation. In getting and setting up a meeting place there are some important things to be aware of:

- How many people are expected? A big room with a whole bunch of chairs can be a downer if the meeting draws few people. Aternatively, a too small place can be frustrating. Particularly if it is a fairly long agenda, we may lose people if they have to stand.

- How is the room for ventilation? We don't want participants nodding off from lack of oxygen.

- Is the lighting sufficient? This is important if people are going to be doing any reading or writing.

- Is there sufficient room to break into small discussion groups if required?

- Is it easy to get to? As well, does everyone know where it is? A place that requires navigation through dark streets might discourage women from attending. Is it accessible for people with disabilities?

- Does it have meaning to the people to be involved - i.e., will the participants feel comfortable and welcome? Sometimes a school or church will appear to have an ideal meeting room but may have a poor reputation among the people that may make them reticent to attend.

- Do we have the equipment needed – flip chart paper or newsprint, marking pens, a black board and chalk, a sound system?

Members of a water development project in Northern Nigeria went out to Fulani women to listen to their concern about water.

Elections

Sooner or later the group with which you are working is going to have to structure itself into some sort of formal democratic organization. Thus, in the great majority of cases, elections are required. This can be a tricky business for a number of reasons:

1. The most well known people may not necessarily be the best folks to have in positions of formal leadership responsibility. They may be popular, but may not have the personal or organizational skills necessary for a new people's organization.

2. There may be people around who have a good deal of experience – in unions or housing co-ops for instance – but that experience may not have been very positive. Remember our discussion of the lack of availability of democratic models. The experienced person may indeed bring a very top-down, elitist view of a community organization or participation.

Example: An environmental group in southern Ontario was in deep trouble – their finances were in terrible shape; they had very little participation; there was a vicious battle being waged between two factions. The recently elected executive sought the services of a community organizer to try to sort things out. In the course of talking with people it became clear that a lot of the difficulty went back about 3 years to the first elected president. He had been very experienced in the movement, but had used this to dominate and browbeat members. He was secretive, effectively fostered conflicts, and discouraged participation. When he left a new group took over – one of the factions – who modeled their behaviour on his actions. They had some important unlearning to do.

3.   Elections can begin a process of subtly splitting the community into in-group and out-group, winners and losers. This can be particularly difficult where there are racial or ethnic differences. Think of the pain and disruption that some feminist organizations have had to go through because they had not attended to issues of women of colour. Thus, the process of who "runs", and how the election is handled, is crucial. It is important to assist the silent majority (or minority) to be heard, and any dominant types to listen.

4.   Elections can suggest to people that the elected folks - the board, the executive - are now the ones that will do all the work and make all decisions. This, of course, can ruin any ethic of participation. As we have seen, genuine participation is a crucial objective of community development. On the other hand, if handled well, elections can begin, or rejuvenate, a democratic and empowering process. Then, if issues are clear, people have a good opportunity to express their views, and positive consensus can be forged; election of leaders will be framed in a positive way.

Organizing Priorities

Within this phase, priorities will become important and perhaps problematic - particularly as money is scarce, and issues emerge as complex and interrelated. Often citizens have to be assisted in organizing their priorities. We need to be clear that when we assist people to develop a needed program in the community, we are not necessarily doing "community development". Community programming can contribute to the development of community but it is not the same thing. Program development involves creation of a concrete benefit that the community needs, but to focus on it exclusively would be to miss the point of developing the community. Thus, a question that we should always be aware of is: "How does this fit with other efforts that are taking place to build a stronger people?". McKnight (1995) makes the point that the development of programs in communities has sometimes undercut other aspects of community life - such as, spontaneous support of one another. Therefore, we need to ask questions such as the following:

- Are we developing leadership as we create and manage the program?

- Does the organization of the program fit the culture of the community?

- Does the community feel ownership of the program?

- Is it the most necessary program, or are there others that are more in need of scarce energy and resources?

It is important that priorities be related to purposes or objectives (Dale, 1978). There are also other considerations:

1. It may be that there is an easy objective which will give people confidence to go on to more difficult ones. This may involve something very possible, what Alinsky calls a "cinch victory" over a particular adversary or difficulty (like reaching a membership quota or gaining a meeting with an important bureaucrat or elected official).

2. On the other hand, the situation may dictate the choice of a difficult objective: for example, some funding may have to be sought
for training before any other part of the program can be insti-
tuted. This type of objective should be avoided at first, if at all
possible, in that it can be a long, technical process that may be
"iffy", has few immediate payoffs, and will involve few people.

3. Sometimes a number of goals or objectives are so interrelated
that it is either easier, or even mandatory, to go after a number of
them at once. Advantages of various courses of action can and
should be pointed out, but not in such a way or at such a pace
that the community people feel left behind or stupid. If the people in the community can do the analysis themselves with only
small assistance from the organizer, the exercise can be even
more productive (i.e., the members are developing their own
skills, confidence and sense of responsibility for their actions).
Popular education techniques, like Root Cause Analysis or Dot-
Mocracy, can be useful in identifying and ranking priorities (Lee
& Balkwill, 1996).

Analyzing Objectives

1. Each objective should be outlined in terms of the necessary strategies, and the resources (first in general, and later in particular)
likely to be needed to carry on a successful program.

2. As well, objectives must be examined in terms of other objectives: how do they influence each other? This will, in large part,
determine whether some objectives can be combined in relation
to strategy, or whether they have to be separated and gone after
one by one.

3. Committees must be set up to investigate and plan the number of
resources necessary for the attainment of particular objectives.
This again will foster analysis, participation, and a proliferation
of leadership roles - a sine qua non of effective organizing!

Maintaining the Organization

I am against the reification of organizations. They are not things. They are people.
—*Matthew Clark (Toronto Disarmament Network)*

1. When must we keep people together?

   • When large numbers are needed.

   • When the organization needs a wide representation. (Remember the question that is almost always asked by the media and opposition, "Whom do you represent?").

   • When key people are needed:
     - because they possess particular skills;
     - because they have credibility within the community;
     - because of the credibility they have within the opposing group or institution or with media.

2. When can the organization afford to lose people?

   • When some are trouble makers:
     - those who are working at cross purposes to the majority;
     - those who are rumour mongers and major gossipers;
     - those who are too impatient and cannot accept the necessary discipline of working collectively;
     - someone who is on an "ego trip".

   • To polarize a situation by serving notice that certain positions or classes, as represented by particular individuals, are not welcome. (Often these are found among the list above). Alinsky (1971) claims that polarization is of major importance in mobilizing people for action.

   • For efficiency: when there are too many people for the tasks at hand.

3.　　Keeping Groups Going:

- Keep in mind that ups and downs in energy and issues' relevance are normal - don't panic during the downs, but be sure to attend to them. Don't get euphoric during the ups – keep working at the basics as well as taking advantage of opportunities.

- Through the "downs", keep the key leaders identified and fueled. Keep an up-to-date list of names of members. Besides leaders there are, at least, three levels of membership. (See Figure 7-1: Activity/Level of Member Commitment).
    - Mailing list types – people who are generally not involved, but who would like to be kept informed. (We might be able to mobilize them later).
    - Active members – people who will come out to meetings, deliver Flyers on occasion, will sign petitions, etc.
    - The committed members – people who will have meetings at their houses, donate money, participate in Fund raising, sit on committees, etc..

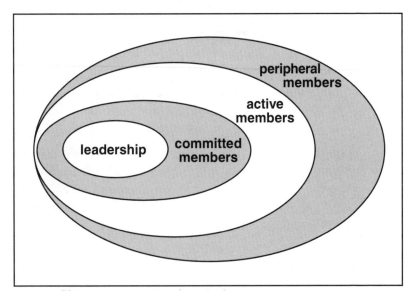

Figure 7-1: Activity/level of member commitment

- Provide workshops, leadership, tactics and communication training, for example.

- Assist members to be always on the lookout for issues that can become the focus for group action – issues that have emotional appeal, are real and imminent.

Example: An organizer, in talking about an energetic campaign being waged by the Parents of Peel organization, pointed out that members had been concerned about a number of issues but that none really seemed to be galvanizing support. "Things had been pretty quiet for awhile. We were working on things but not with any great energy. Suddenly, we happened on the issue of mold in portable classrooms - the mold seemed to be causing some real health problems. This galvanized a lot of interest. We didn't know it was there at first; we were just looking at various issues and this one - the health of the kids - hit a public nerve; and not just with parents, but with environmentalists and teachers too. Sometimes you just have to keep poking at various issues".

- Avoid the trap of being a narrow issue organization; that may solve one problem, but does little to come together to develop power to influence its environment in the long run.

- Make sure meetings are productive and as much fun as possible. Head off "busy work" meetings.

- Keep trying for small victories or achievements, and keep the members informed.

- Ensure that enthusiastic leaders are not taking on too much for their strength or abilities, or pushing volunteers too hard. Watch for "burnout"; for example, a suddenly developed short temper, habitual complaints about members, defeatist attitude – "yes we can try that, but I don't think it has much of a chance"; forgotten appointments, etc. (Cruikshank, 1989).

- Help the leadership maintain openness to citizens – flexibility.

- Have some fun event like a party or dance.

Planning

Planning is the process of developing structures, programs and actions for the attainment of a particular objective or objectives, through the development and the allocation of scarce resources: e.g., people, money.

The people who are to carry out the plan must be involved to the maximum. (Remember the participation objective). The better a plan is understood, the better it will be implemented. The more someone has participated in the planning of something, the more that person will want to see it implemented, and have a stake in its success.

At this point, the expertise of the organizer is still of importance, but she has to stress clearly that it is the members' plan and thus up to them to carry out. It is their concrete interests that are involved here. It can be a tricky business, attempting to impart important consultation or direction while at the same time staying "behind the scenes", not taking from the people the responsibility of the planning task (Speeter, 1978). The victory - or what the American Organizer, Heather Booth, calls "the struggle" - must be with and by the people (1974: 4).

Most of the planning will be done in committees, the most important vehicle for participation, and brought back to the larger "official group" for examination, criticism and ratification.

If elections are necessary (in a standing committee, for example), they can be frequent - even every six to eight months is not totally out of the question at the beginning of work, or if there has been a fair turnover in membership. This gives a number of people the opportunity to be involved, and to try out leadership roles.

Sessions should not occur too far apart, or be held sporadically. It is crucial to maintain enthusiasm, and a sense of coherence and purpose, through what can be a long, drawn-out, exacting process.

Training

More often than not, training is going to be necessary at more than one point in the group's life. It may be necessary to learn, for example:

* how to communicate better in small groups;

* program planning - which might include priority or problem-solving skills; some models of planning, or approaches to problem solving; and budgeting

* decision-making styles - this is often crucial in assisting the organization to achieve and maintain a democratic stance. It looks so much easier on the surface to have one or a few persons make decisions (remember our pyramidal models); it may be necessary to do some reflection and have some practice in order to see the value of consensus and democratic styles of decision-making. It might be a good idea, in this instance, to try a rotating chair model.

While keeping in mind that phases are rarely discrete, whatever is necessary should occur between planning and implementation phases of any particular strategy. The organizer usually has some training skills, but if she does not, some attempts should be made to bring in someone. This will often require money. Training is a critical aspect of community organizing. Since it may cost money it is often down-played or sometimes ignored. A well-planned strategy can easily fail if the people who are to carry it off are insufficiently grounded in the basics of what they have to do.

> **Example**: The Affordable Housing Action Association was building a tenants organizing campaign in Mississauga, Ontario. They brought in George Lakey (the well known U.S. trainer and writer) to lead a workshop on Direct Action strategies. Not only did he impart new knowledge, but his ability to connect the local struggle to some of his experiences with other groups provided the AHAA people with inspiration and energy. Training can provide more to a group than information.

Funding

An organization may decide that it needs money for some particular program or task. Ideally it is preferable for a group of people to accomplish what they can with volunteer labour because:

1. If some folks are getting paid while others are not, envy and dissension can result; the organization might lose some people or waste energy on personal infighting.

    Example: There was a horrible example in southern Ontario. What had been a very effective anti-poverty group, after about a year and a half obtained sufficient funding to hire a couple of the members as staff. The salary was to last only a year and was set at minimum wage. Nevertheless, one of the key members, who had applied unsuccessfully for one of the positions, became jealous. She used her position on the board to make life miserable for the two women who were now working for the organization. Eventually her behaviour became so dysfunctional that other board members had to ask her to resign.

2. Voluntarism will clearly provide the sense that the group has struggled for something and won.

3. There is always the danger that a "culture of funding" may result - i.e., that only through funded programs can things get done. Further, the search for funding may come to monopolize the activity and energy of the organization – i.e., the organization's life may come to be the primary goal rather than the issue(s) it was set up to deal with. (Pivan and Cloward, 1978: xxii)

Now, having made our case against the search for funding, it is clear that often it is essential – training has been mentioned, essential travel may demand money, an office with telephones and fax machines, and other concurrent administrative costs may have to be established, etc..

In going after funding it can be helpful to:

1. Indicate the amount of volunteer time the organization has, particularly in reference to the task for which dollars are being sought. Some funders require proof that we are already doing things - eg., settlement integration of immigrant - before they will offer funding. Thus, we will need to have some form of record-keeping structure/process to justify need. They will want to see that we had people volunteering in the area. It is a good leverage on a potential funder. Also, this can give people a psychological lift when they see how much, and how important, their time has been.

2. Make a point of being clear on the priorities of the potential funders. It is demoralizing for people to spend a lot of time filling out the required forms, only to be told that our organization or request doesn't fall within the criteria. Often we can get annual reports or outlines that will be helpful.

3. Be careful of tailoring the request only to the funder's criteria. It is dangerous to set objectives which someone from outside of the community sees as important. On the other hand, we may be able to frame the language of a proposal that will sound good to a funder and maintain the objectives of the group's project. Be creative.

4. Ensure that our group understands funding process and forms. Incomplete information annoys funders. Often this is the only connection bureaucrats will have with an organization, so be attentive.

5. Ensure that the funding criteria are absolutely clear. Get, or give, a letter outlining our understanding of what has been given to us verbally. This can save us frustration, and keep your group from being accused of fiddling with the books. Watch for the problem of: "We don't fund X, but if you can get X funded we will fund Y and Z".

6.   Any people receiving funding should clearly possess the skills to do the job. When money is obtained there is always the temptation to use it to reward loyal and hard working people. This can be problematic if it appears that "insiders" are scratching each other's backs; it is important to not only be a just and equitable organization, but to appear to be so.

Example: The Single Mothers Against Poverty Group developed a creative way to handle some of the problems of funding when they received a summer employment grant. Instead of "hiring staff", they wrote up a list of tasks that needed to be done and put a dollar value to each one – typing a letter $X.00; attending a community meeting, $X.00; etc. In this way all members got a chance to be reimbursed a little for jobs that they were doing. No one got rich, but no one got jealous either.

7.   Realize that funding staff and project officers, particularly from big funders - government foundations or the United Way - are often used to dealing with large formal bureaucracies. They may have little experience with community-based organizations, and may need education as to the differences and advantages of such organizations.

Example: A grassroots project in Uganda, of women dealing with AIDS issues, faced the dilemma of a funder who demanded an evaluation process before releasing dollars for a second phase of the project. There were two problems: the women realized that they needed to spend energy on a needs assessment that would involve the members of their project. (This off-shore evaluation process, while perhaps useful for the funder, had a negative impact on their members - it would divert limited energy away from mobilization of local communities); the evaluation process had been developed in North America, and the women found that it did not connect well with their experience and culture. For some time the women and project officer wrangled over the issue. Finally, the problem was resolved when the members went ahead and did their own needs assessment and sent the results into the head office in Canada. The funder accepted it as an interim report, but suggested that the evaluation would have to be done sooner or later. A good deal of energy and time had been spent on a funder rather than community issues.

8. Remember that funders, particularly government, prefer to fund services over advocacy or organizing. At the very least, they will want us to delineate and priorize each of these activities as different functions. Unfortunately the organizing life of community-based groups does not run along such clear, separate lines. Chaos is often the rule, and it is difficult to predict whether advocacy or organizing will be the focus at any given time. Thus, a worker who is funded to do program development may find herself in a situation where she may be involved in advocacy action - situations like this won't wait until there is a free day in program development.

Example: When (in 1995) the right-wing Conservative government was elected in the province of Ontario, one of the first things they did was to tell project officers not to fund any proposals that had the terms "community development" or "advocacy" in them. Their view was, apparently, that they did not wish to assist voices that would raise objections to their agenda of making war on the poor and marginalized. Proposals had to be presented in a very cautious manner. Even so, many useful programs lost their funding, and money and resources disappeared from many communities and important causes.

Some other considerations on funding:

Corporate Funding
If there is a particular project in mind that might lend itself to corporate sponsorship – hiring a fundraiser or buying a van to transport children, seniors or disabled people, for example – it may be worth looking directly to the private companies. If so:

1.   Try to get funding for more than a year. It is not unlikely that with the vagaries of the economy, subsequent requests will be met with less than an enthusiastic response.

2.   Try to put three or four requests together so that:
   • If one doesn't come through it isn't too damaging.
   • The company understands that it isn't being expected to "carry the load" by itself.

3.   Check out the kind of project that the company is supporting. Don't waste time on places that have no interest in the kinds of things your groups are doing.

4.   Send the proposal to the chief executive officer (call to find out who it is). However, don't expect to deal with the CEO.

5.   Call and find out exactly what they want in a proposal. Don't waste time by giving them extraneous information, or waste their time and ours making them ask for stuff you have left out of your submission.

6.   If the group can be registered as a charitable organization – companies want that tax break. (You cannot do this in Canada if your organization has a so-called "political" purpose, which the government tends to interpret in very broad terms)

7.   If successful, be sure to:
   • Call and thank them.
   • Send them a report on how the money was used.

8.   It can be helpful to get to them early on, or late in their fiscal year, when they have lots of money or some left over.

   Note: Do not get connected with a company that has caused or is causing problems for the community. Be sure that the community is consulted if some company offers resources. There can be exceptions to this rule. In fighting the James Bay Hydro project the Cree received company transportation help a few times. However, it was always made clear that there were no favours in return. (McGregor, 1989)

Foundations

1. Again, be sure to get to them early enough in their fiscal year so we don't miss out; and take a crack at them late in the year to check if they have any money left over.

2. If turned down, try to find out "why", so that a better approach may be taken next time by your group.

3. It is often preferable to try for a three year strategy. We may be better off than with a one shot deal.

4. Be prepared to educate the funder. For example, the foundation may not understand that an organization cannot pay for a van out of its general operating budget if one has United Way funding. Another example is that funders are often not aware that the Department of Indian Affairs in Canada does not fund off-reserve organizations.

Service Clubs

1. Usually there are limited funds available ($50.00 - $1,500.00).

2. Keep in mind that these clubs are usually inundated by requests.

3. Requests often work best if the service club can take on the group as a project.

4. Local contacts can be important. It can be helpful if a member of their group can be involved with your group in some way.

Trade Union Movement

1. Best requests are around particular social issues (e.g., racism, equal pay or day care).

2. Sometimes they give money (or "in kind" assistance).

   Example: A teacher's organization in southern Ontario provided money to a group that was attempting to organize parents around the issue of the quality of education resources and steep government cut backs. This allowed the group to acquire a part-time organizer and really expand its activities.

3.　　Sometimes they give consultation.

> **Example**: A small union that was on strike received a loan of a labour negotiator. He was very helpful at both negotiating and teaching. With the skills learned from him, they were able to be more effective in future negotiating situations.

Direct Mail (or Direct Contact) Campaigns

1.　　Usually this is aimed at our own constituency. Usually these are people who support, or are in some way connected to, the issue.

2.　　We can only expect small amounts from each person.

3.　　A great many requests are needed, as the response rate is usually about 1-3 per cent. This can be boosted to 5-6 per cent with careful targeting (a quite sophisticated process). It can also help to carefully craft the "begging letter". In this regard it is useful to:

- Keep the message short, clear and to the point. Long letters are simply not read.

- Connect our message to the interests of our potential donors. How does our cause affect them?

- Insofar as possible, use the language of your potential donors. That is, don't use jargon or revolutionary rhetoric or talk down to them. They need to feel a kinship with the people that are asking for the assistance.

4.　　With technology becoming more affordable, computerized mailing lists are very helpful. Sometimes groups will share their lists with us if we can do something for them – free advertising if our group has a newsletter, for example.

5.　　After three weeks, do not expect any more responses.

6.　　Supermarkets will sometimes be prepared to put request material with the grocery bags. The same is true of laundromats and churches.

7.   Other groups, which are similarly disposed to ours, might be doing mailings onto which we can piggy-back.

8.   It can take some time but it can be very helpful to develop a support or "Friends Of..." group that will do some fund raising for you. These would be people who do not have much interest in grassroots organizing, but who see the utility of our organization and are prepared to organize an event, or lend their names to a fund raising campaign.

Dealing With Internal Opposition

A question that can be very important in this phase (and at other times as well) is: Is there in the general community, at least, a passive willingness for change in relation to the major problems or some particular problem? At least there must be no powerful person or group in the community who will actively resist action toward change. There may well be some, possibly a majority, who are indifferent; but, basically, they can be left (not ignored) for the time being, until it is in their interest to become involved. There will be members, though, who will resist change - as Paulo Friere says, they resist change because they either fear power; they have a conservative notion of how the community should look and operate; they have an interest (ties to power elites) in maintaining the status quo; or they do not trust other members sufficiently to share power within their own community (big egos). We will have to deal with them. We will probably already have picked up information on them in our private research. We (and the members) will have to develop some strategies for getting them to change, for neutralizing them, and/or for going around them in some way.

There are a number of principles to keep in mind when developing a strategy to do any of the above:

1.   **The strategy must not divide the community or must divide it as little as possible.** (Remember we may have to lose someone, and that may mean alienating their friends.) The people must gain strength from the exercise. It is not uncommon for

communities to have a history of internal civil wars. Past history can breed some bad habits – quick reactions, rumour mongering, character assassination – and that can make it difficult for the members to come together in a positive atmosphere. (Remember our discussion of "frustration instigated behaviour'). It is important, in so far as it is humanly possible, to stress the commonalities among members, and help them see and accept opportunities to come together.

Example: A housing co-op was attempting to get the city to do something about drivers speeding through its grounds as a shortcut to a major road. There was real danger for kids. The community was unfortunately split on tactics. The executive wanted to move slowly. Some concerned parents wanted to take direct action (perhaps a barricade across the co-op entrance). The executive appeared to be fearful of angering the city bureaucrats and were stalling. Members of the parent group became so frustrated that they appeared at a board meeting and began to publicly berate the Chairman, accusing him of not caring about kids and of being a power monger. From that point on the issue became personalized. Two sides formed around the personalities involved, and many issues became subsumed by "whose side are you on?". While the issue with the city was eventually solved, a year later the co-op was still dealing with the conflict.

It is useful, in this context, to reflect back on one of the key role demands on an organizer - that of mediator. When possible, we need to be prepared to take on the responsibility of getting people to at least negotiate (a key skill) with each other. It will not always be successful, but it is our responsibility to consider and attempt it before events travel too far down an "us/them" divide.

2. **The strategy and objective will be partially determined by the understanding we and our group have of the reasons for resistance.**[2] For example, if a person has strong ties with the opposition, it is likely that tactics will be aimed at neutralizing or overcoming rather than changing. If a person is unclear about group vision or objectives, some sort of clarifying or teaching will have to be done.

3. **Do not be in too much of a hurry to totally resolve the situation** unless the person has sufficient clout to immediately stop positive action. Time can achieve many things, with a little assistance. Sometimes a slow groundswell of activity within a community can eventually bring the opposition around to becoming first line advocates for militancy and change. Sometimes the opposition simply gets left behind by events and the people.

4. As Alinsky says, whatever one decides to do about the problem, **the tactic must be within the experience of the people.** Also, we must move at the community's pace.

5. In that vein, always try to negotiate first.

6. **It must be nonviolent.** This is important; in the heat of the moment, someone may want to "take a shot" at the person or persons who are standing in the way of the community's wishes. This would not only raise ethical problems; it can backfire and cause others to back away from our organization (seeing it as undisciplined or prone to violence).

7. If confrontation is necessary, whatever one does, it is important to place and keep the person or people resisting on the defensive. However carefully the people must be handled, we need to keep their negative position clear (explaining their position and accounting for its shortcomings). They must be kept off balance so that they cannot spend time attacking our group's position. In short, we have to keep the argument within our perspective.

8. If things really get confrontational, it is also important to heighten the awareness of the community as to the differences between that person and the rest of the community - i.e., polarize the situation. This doesn't mean that we have to make her look like "the bad guy" (though it may); it is, however, important for the community to see their interests as differing from hers. In short, the person's credibility on this issue - not on all issues - must be undermined.

9. Always do our best to keep links of communication open and clear. We want to be amenable to any positive move as well as ready to combat any negative tactics.

Reflection

There are lots of problems to be faced and dealt with, and people can become either totally transfixed with organizational maintenance; or equally bored by the minutiae. These are dangers that must be faced, and dealt with creatively and sensitively. In a sense, a community organization must be able to re-invent itself as it responds to the unique and complex forces and situations it faces. It is worth the work. Organization development is a crucial objective and phase for community workers. It is the base from which coherent action will spring.

Endnotes

[1] For more on building and maintaining people's organizations see Lakey et al. (1995), *Grassroots and Non-profit Leadership*; and/or Gastil (1993) *Democracy in Small Groups*. Lee and Balkwill's (1996) *Participatory Planning for Action* offers a number of popular education exercises that are very useful in identifying action targets and planning strategy.

[2] Early in Chapter 8 we will look at a way of analyzing the terrain of support and opposition in relation to action.. The principles there are fairly applicable here as well.

**ORGANIZATIONAL DEVELOPMENT
PHASE SUMMARY**

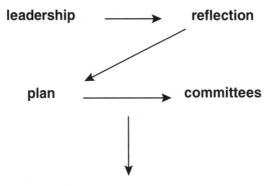

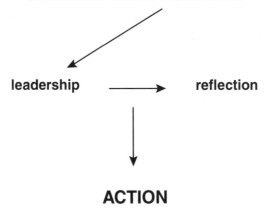

Chapter

8

POPULAR ACTION

Never doubt that a small group of thoughtful,
committed individuals can change the world
- it is the only thing that ever has.
                                    —*Margaret Mead*

Treating action as a separate topic is somewhat artificial. Clearly, the organizer and organization have been active for some time. Indeed, some of what is to follow - which tends to be focused on external community support and resistance - could be utilized in intra-community support building. However, as indicated in the last chapter, we will reach a point where the externally focused action is or should be more direct, as well as more clearly in the hands of the people. This is what the whole exercise has been about in the first place: people taking responsibility, or putting their new-found skills and confidence into action.

The nature of community development - the attempt to reorder power and alter the pattern of resource allocation - tells us, that as well as mobilizing like minded friends, community groups will find themselves facing serious resistance on any number of occasions. Elites are simply not going to do things that they see as detrimental to the maintenance of their privileged positions. As well, as movement activists remind us, it is not simply the "other side" that we have to influence (Moyer, 1987). Social issues are complex, and the terrain in which we are working will have an array of groups that take various positions about the issue we are attempting to deal with - we need to be able to analyze the landscape. The following section provides a framework to guide strategy.

Understanding and Addressing Levels of Support and Opposition

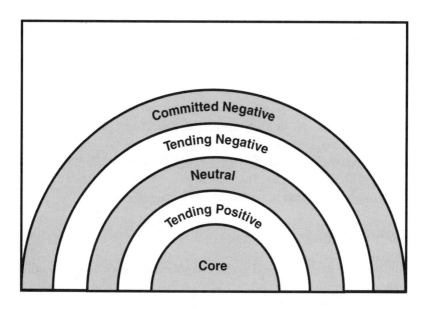

Figure 8-1: Levels of Support and Opposition

If we are facing resistance, there are typically two broad groups that we tend to identify: those for us, and those against us. If the issue is very important we may think of them as "the good guys" and "the bad guys". As far as rhetoric goes, it is rather nice to maintain these divisions. Life, however, is rarely so simple; and if we are going to have any chance at gaining our points, it is important that we develop a more sophisticated notion of the ground upon which our struggles are played out. The analysis in the model presented here is one aspect of strategy development. What we want to do is to analyze the various tendencies that occur when there are two opposing points of view. As we can see in Figure 8-1 (Levels of Support and Opposition), we can loosely divide the field into five groups: those who are committed to the cause; those sympathetic; those neutral; those tending to be unsympathetic to our cause, or sympathetic to the cause of the opposition; and finally, those committed to opposing our cause. In developing a strategy for dealing with opposition, all positions will have to be considered and a number of issues will need attention.

Since popular groups rarely have unlimited resources, it is important that we use resources that we do have for the greatest impact. Thus, it is important when dealing with opposition that we understand clearly whom we are dealing with, and how these people relate to our group's objectives and why. Following such an analysis, it will be clearer to us how to act - with or on them. With this in mind, let us examine the categories from a few important perspectives: the type of people in each group; their reasons for supporting, resisting or hesitating; the resources that each group has available to influence others; and the tactics we may be able to use to deal with each group .

Core Group

This group certainly would include community leadership and core activists. There may be others who - for reasons of self-interest or solidarity - will enthusiastically work with our group in what we want to do or achieve.

> **Example:** New Orleans activist Louise Martin became involved in a struggle to block the creation of a massive warehouse store in a Black community near to her family's home. She was concerned both as a "neighbour" of that community (self-interest), and as one who had concern about the negative impact the development would have for all the people who lived in the "Garden District" of the city (solidarity).

These folks will constitute a major part of the resources available for carrying through our strategy: they come to all the meetings; and they may have social relationships outside of community business (though this is not necessary). They tend to contribute ideas and time, and possibly resources (like money, specific expertise or contacts with elites).

For these folks it is important that:

- we understand their motivations;
- they have good communication among themselves;
- they know what to do;
- they be kept well informed;
- they have good support (they are doing a big job).

Swing Group Tending Positive

These are people who, the strategy team knows, are supportive in general, though the extent of that support may be unclear. They generally see their interests and values bound up with those of the core group, or the population that the core group represents; but are hesitating for some reason. So we need to be clear on:

What causes their positive motivations:

- How are they connected to the issue?

- Are they personally affected? Sometimes there is a person-to-person relationship that tends to draw someone toward supporting our position. Is there a personal loyalty to a committed member or members?

- A third possibility is that a person or group is generally ideologically sympathetic to the position of your group.

Why are they hesitating?

- Do they have some kind of connection to the other side? Personal loyalties can swing both ways, and a person or group may hesitate because they happen to respect people who nevertheless are against us.

- Are they concerned with some aspect of our campaign?
  -Is our rhetoric needlessly putting some people off?

  Example: In the winter 1994-95 occupation of the Revenue Canada Offices by First Nation groups protesting treaty violations, some supporters (Native and White) were alarmed when one of the women elders read out a statement that included an implication that the protesters might use violence. This was unacceptable to most of us and we immediately sought clarification that this was an error. (It was.)

- Do they have an incorrect, or unclear, idea of what the issue is about? This is not uncommon as many disputes involve complex aspects which the media tend to oversimplify or misrepresent.

Whatever the issue they are not acting. We need to keep them supportive and perhaps move them into a more active relationship. Thus we need to:

- Understand their motivations and concerns;
- Develop information and arguments for them based on those motivations and concerns;
- Provide them with opportunities for action;
- Negotiate with them (what do they need in order to become more helpful?);
- Keep in communication with them and support them.

Neutral Group

These people are usually the most numerous. They are the folks who say, "I can't be bothered." or "Well, both sides have their points". Many times they are folks who fear the conflict inherent to the issue, and they either try to avoid it or not recognize it - "I just don't know what all the fuss is about". They may, on the other hand, be genuinely unclear on the issues; or have some relationships with people on both sides. With this group we need to:

- Try to understand their concerns about the core position and the opposition position;

- Help them to find common ground with our position, and be prepared to negotiate to increase that common ground;

  Example: A Toronto community group was fighting a "block busting" landlord who was turning good low income apartment housing into "dumps". He was trying to force his present tenants to leave so he could develop the buildings as high rent condos. The small group desperately needed the help of the local ratepayer organization to put pressure on city council, and the by-law enforcement department, to take action. Most of the ratepayer executive were neutral: they didn't want to take sides because the people at risk were tenants, not home owners. The activists had no luck in talking them into getting involved, though the organizer was able to get the ratepayer's president to go through the building to see the conditions people were being forced to live in - holes in the walls and ceiling, no hot water, etc.. When the little delegation got there, the owner turned up and attempted to block the entrance. He and the president got into quite a heated argument and some pushing and shoving took place. This incident convinced the president that the group deserved support against this nasty person and he was instrumental in getting the ratepayers to take action to assist the tenants.

- If we cannot move them into sympathy, figure out what we can do to keep them on the fence;

- Keep the line of communication open.

Swing Group Tending Negative

These are people who generally see their interests and principles bound to the opposition. As well, they may have important relationships there. They also, of course, may be quite misinformed about the issues. They may be interested in taking action against your project but are not looking for a fight. Our emphasis with this group is to try to move them to a more neutral position. Thus it is important to:

- Try to understand their motivations and concerns;

- Develop arguments which negate concerns and enhance motivations;

- Look for issues and personalities that can move them away from the opposition and toward the core;

- Be prepared to negotiate with them if the possibility arises;

- Avoid stirring them up if possible.

Committed Opposition

These are our opposition. They have interests in opposition to the position of the community with which we are working. They will be working hard to attempt to defeat our group. They will have their own networks which they will be using to develop a strategy, part of which will be to do the very things we are recommending in this section. The basic approach here is, at least in the short range to isolate, not convince them. With these people it is important to:

- Not underestimate them; but not become totally focused on their negativity either;

- Develop clarity as to their objectives, and keep our analysis of their strategy sharp;

- Plan counter strategies and tactics;

- Keep lines of communication open so that we can negotiate with them if possible.

As Moyer (1987) points, out there are three aspects to action, and each has to do with gaining or maintaining public support.

1. Alerting the public to the issue or problem;

2. Convincing a majority, or a significant minority, that it is an issue worthy of support;

3. Offering a convincing alternative for the resolution of the issue.

It is to the public we must often make our case, not the committed opposition.

Organizational Linkages

We spoke in the last chapter about developing an organization as an aspect of building our capacity for action. Sometimes it becomes important to connect our organization with others to increase that action potential. Our group may need to link with other organizations - either within the community or outside of it. There are two main reasons why this can be useful:

1. We may need to gain resources that our group cannot hope to acquire;

   Example: Chetwynd, the Toronto-based community organization project that works with assisted housing communities, focuses on assisting residents to strengthen local networks, and to identify community issues on which they wish to work. There are ongoing attempts to connect with both existing community organizations (such as a residents' association and public service organizations). The project has fairly limited resources; so, through linkages, they feel they can increase the resources that can be made available to the community, while helping to improve the quality of relationships between the community and service providers.

2.   We may discover a like-minded organization, which is fighting for issues that have relevance to our group's struggles (e.g. Community planning organizations sometimes join with Labour groups to advocate on behalf of the poor and marginalized).

Types of Linkages

1. Liaisons. Sometimes different organizations identify a couple of their own people to help keep each other informed of the events and plans each group develops. In this case it is simply a matter of maintaining a good communication line with the other group. We do not meld our organizations or processes, but try to coordinate certain activities and information.

Another form of liaising involves having people from one organization sit on the board of another. Again, it is not uncommon to find representatives of Labour groups sitting on boards of community planning organizations.

2. Coalitions. In this case we are joining formally with another group, or groups, and agreeing to take joint action on specific issues. We are creating an "umbrella" organization, to which we agree to contribute resources - one which will speak and act for us on the identified issues. We may integrate some activities, and often become part of a group to decide strategies and tactics. We do not, however, give up our own specific identity; and we will continue to work, by ourselves, on issues of our unique concern. There are several examples of this kind of linkage between First Nations, peace, and environmental movements; as well as with anti-poverty groups. A coalition allows us to focus resources and effort on larger issues with which many groups also identify.

Youth taking part in a Days of Action protest against the policies of the right-wing Ontario government. These Days of Action campaigns, which occurred at various cities throughout Ontario, are examples of coalitions of a large number of groups.

Example: When an Ontario Native group started to resist the Canadian Federal government on its attempt to break treaty rights regarding taxation, a number of groups came together to contribute to the effort of the "Revenue Rez" occupation in Toronto. One organization leader became the spokesperson for the whole group, though all groups were involved in decisions concerning how to develop the protest and how to get the message out to the general public.

3. Mass-based Organizations. These are a type of coalition, and ones which were popularized by Alinsky in the 1950's and 1960's. In this case, small local organizations come together and form a new "super-organization" under one elected leadership. This organization is mandated to deal with the issues agreed upon, and the leadership develops strategy and acts for the organization. The member organizations continue to carry out their own activities on issues not covered by the MBO. Examples of MBO's can be seen in the work of Saul Alinsky with the Woodlawn Organization in Chicago (Horwitt 1989, Alinsky 1970).

4. Amalgamation. In this case we decide that two or more groups must come together and give up their identity as separate groups. This can come about in a situation where all groups involved are so focused on the same issue that it makes no sense to maintain separate organizations. It may also occur where one or more groups has lost steam and cannot continue with any sense of effectiveness.

In entering into any one of these organizational relationships, we need to be clear about what we are gaining as well as what we are giving up. We need to understand clearly the organizational culture and values of the other folks, so that we do not get into unnecessary philosophical or strategic wrangles. We also need to be clear and open about our own culture and values so that the other group(s) will be in a similarly informed position.

There are a few questions we can ask when examining which, if any, organizational linkage is appropriate for our group:

1.   What is the vision of the organization with which we are negotiating a linkage?

2.   How clear is the other organization on what we are about?

3.   What resources are involved - from us, or for us?

4.   How important is our autonomy?

5.   Is this a long term situation, of a one-off activity?

6.   Who is going to be responsible for the activity of bringing the linkage into being?

The answers to these questions can assist us in figuring out the path to, or away from, forming a particular organizational linkage.

Demonstrations

We are defining demonstration, broadly, as any public event that will bring positive attention to the issues we are raising. At some point, in most organizing situations, there may be a need for some sort of public display. This is particularly true in contest situations, but may be important for any organizing endeavor. Rallies, marches, street dances, concerts, community fairs, or fun runs are examples of demonstrations.

1.   Why Demonstrate?

a)   *For publicity.* The group may merely want to call attention to its existence: what its problems are, or what it is trying to do for the community. On the other hand, it may wish to call attention to what someone, or some institution, is doing to the community.

Members of the Affordable Housing Action Association (Mississauga) begin their campaign against a corporation which had been swindling low income tenants.

b)   *For internal morale.* The group may need to show community members that the members can be mobilized, can pull something off successfully. This may range from putting on a street fair, to calling a press conference, to putting on a mass protest.

> **Example:** In the early 90's the Big Cove First Nation in New Brunswick had experienced a terrible suicide epidemic. In 9 weeks eight young men had taken their lives. The population (about 1800) was in shock. While there were many problems facing the people - racism, unemployment, and a cycle of abuse, for example - leaders understood that they had to demonstrate that the community could do something constructive for itself. They chose to mount a "Mourning and Healing Week" (Lee, 1993). They organized ceremonies, brought in Elders and healers from around North America, and outlawed alcohol from the reserve for the time of the event. Many community members recognized the importance of coming together and publicly sharing their grief and determination to face their problems. Interestingly the epidemic of suicides ceased.

c)   *To show the person or institution, from whom it is trying to extract something, that it does indeed represent a high number of people, and/or that it can garner media attention.*

> **Example:** A small community organization in Metro Toronto has a "community fair" every spring. There are a variety of events – face painting, concerts, clowns and a huge garage sale where neighbourhood folks buy tables at a very reasonable cost and sell used goods. It is well publicized and people come from all over the area. This event raises money which the community group uses the rest of the year, mostly for children's programs. It is interesting that this event invariably draws the local mayor and councillors, who always make a point that they "support" the community. Interestingly, this organization is seen as one of the more influential in the municipality, and one of the few that is routinely kept well informed by politicians as to what is going on at city hall.

d) *To disrupt the operation of the opposition.* This is most commonly found in relation to a union picketing during a strike, and when there has been no success in moving management at the bargaining table (sometimes it is used to get management to come to the bargaining table). However, it is used by other groups as well: Greenpeace actions against sealing and nuclear tests; the Native blockades and occupations for treaty rights; and the United Farm Workers grape boycott pickets, for example.

Example: The Friends of the Lubicon, a support group for the Lubicon Cree Nation's struggle in Alberta, has taken on the multinational resource company Daishowa. That company has been threatening the ancestral lands of the Lubicon with logging. The "Friends" have mounted a long campaign which has included the development of a boycott of businesses that use Daishowa products (like Pizza Pizza). This pizza company had to be picketed and leafleted for months before it finally agreed to join the boycott of Daishowa products (paper bags in this case). (Beedaujahmowin)[1]

e) *All of the above.* More often than not there will be multiple reasons for putting on a demonstration. One good example is: the "unofficial" women's conference on the Canadian constitution in 1981, after the official one had been canceled by the government. It was effective in gaining publicity for women's issues, embarrassing the government (particularly the Secretary of State), and showing everyone just what women could achieve.

Example: The Mohawk standoff at Kanehsatake in 1990 drew a great deal of attention to Canadian First Nations' grievances. It also demonstrated what they could accomplish. Further, when the Surite du Quebec and then the Canadian military moved so violently, it unmasked the oppressive nature of national policy against Native People.[2]

2.   Principles

a)   *Nonviolence.* This is definitely a first principle. If we are ultimately searching seriously for a world where all life is sacred, we have to take note of the dismal failures in this regard - movements where violence has been espoused. The use of violence clearly sanctions violence in the opposition, no matter what lofty aims are advocated. In the words of Walter Wink (Christian scripture scholar and nonviolence advocate): "Violence simply is not radical enough, since it generally changes only the actors but not the way power is exercised" (Desroches 1996). The medium is the message. There is a tremendous pressure and provocation to use physical violence against our fellow human beings but it must be resisted so that we do not merely end up, as Freire would say, mirroring the oppressor. While they are few in number, there are some compelling people after whom we can model our behaviour – Caesar Chavez, Gandhi, Martin Luther King Jr., and (generally) the Suffragettes.[3]

b)   *Stay outside the opposition's experience.* This principle, popularized so well by Saul Alinsky (1970) can be (and increasingly is) a tall order, as everyone's experience is broadened through the media. However, keeping the other side off balance has important payoffs:

- It lets them feel their vulnerability;
- It tends to lead them to respond in ways with which they are unfamiliar.

Example: Even old tactics that haven't been seen for a while can have good effects. The use of sit-ins, by students in universities across North America in the late 60's and early 70's, was successful in part because initially the university administrations would overreact - call in police and refuse to meet with the demonstrators. It is interesting to note that in 1995 the same scenario was played out by First Nations people who took over the Federal Revenue offices in Toronto to protest treaty violations. The occupation lasted 30 days and generated some good publicity.

c) *Stay within the experience of the community.* This is another principle that is strongly recommended by Alinsky (1970). It is a corollary of the above (b), and is rather like the old social work principle, "move at the client's pace". No matter how tempting it is to pull off something that will really grab media attention or which will really stun the other side, it must also be something which will not violate the taste, ethics, or sensibilities of the members of the community.

Example: In 1969 the Just Society (an organization fighting for the rights of Ontario welfare recipients) had a television confrontation with the government Minister John Yremko. The confronters, single support mothers, decided to represent themselves as strong determined women who would not be pushed around. They had solid facts and made forceful statements. Unfortunately, a couple of the women got excited, and started to shout and swear at the minister. Yremko just sat there looking like an innocent cherub under siege by maniacs. People in general, welfare recipients in particular, were not used to this kind of behaviour and not ready to see authority figures treated quite so disrespectfully. It might be different now, after a number of years and scandals have passed, but given the mores of the time, government ministers could not be sworn at in public. The women, in attempting to strengthen their image and prove how unafraid they were, succeeded in turning off their own constituents as well as the Liberals (whose support they wished to maintain).

d) *Discipline.* A public display should always be disciplined. People should be clear on what to do, where to do it, and how it is to be done. This does not mean that spontaneity is out, or that people should not enjoy themselves. Nevertheless, the spontaneity and fun have to occur within some sort of coherent framework - the most loose and enjoyable demonstrations are often the ones that have been planned with the most care. A demonstration cannot simply be a bunch of people informally getting together to celebrate or demand something; it must have a focus, an agenda. Speakers should be given time slots (who will follow whom), and time frames (how long they should speak). It is especially important to make sure speakers stay on the relevant topic.

e) *Novelty.* Campaigns for significant change are rarely short. The higher the stakes, the more difficult it is to convince a community that it can do something, or an opposition that it must do something. Thus, it is important that, whatever kinds of public display the group puts on, they should not be allowed to grow stale. Innovation is important over the long haul, so that people don't feel like they are in a rut. Similarly, if the group is going against a tough adversary, tactics used with great frequency come to be expected and easily countered. Obviously, in a strike, picketing is going to have to be an everyday affair; however, who pickets where, the organizing of "monster" rallies, and diversions on the picket line can alter the rhythm somewhat.

Example: During the "Revenue Rez" 30 day occupation of the Federal Revenue offices, organizers put on a series of events, drumming, a Christmas celebration, even a weekend pow wow. These culture-based activities gave participants a strong sense of community, and generated some great publicity.

f) *Relevant Opposition.* In any public display against an intransigent institution or person, it is important to be clear on the connection between your action, the objective you have, and the opposition itself. Pivan and Cloward make the point that successful protest can only take place if the protesters have some relationship with the protest: "work in his factories, buy his products, go to his school or live in his apartments" (1978: 21). The focus of any action should be the person or body who can make change happen, not merely the handiest target (Dale 1978:).

Example: Social workers and teachers in Ontario, who have struck against their employers, are often told by these agencies that it is not the agency's fault, and they should be dealing with government - the body that develops funding and policy. The correct response has always been: "Yes, but we work for you. Negotiate fairly with us and we'll help you develop strategies to deal with government". Social workers and teachers rarely have direct access to government. Their leverage is only with their employers. (See Pivan and Cloward's Poor Peoples Movements, Chapter 1).

g)   *Secondary Targets.* Having noted the above example, it is often possible to find secondary targets who, if lobbied or threatened with action, might put some pressure on the primary target. Native groups concerned with pollution have been reasonably successful at this - particularly in getting churches to lobby companies in which they have stock. Secondary targets then can be relevant potential target groups, providing they have some leverage on the primary target.

Example: A group of ex-psychiatric patients, fighting to get decent housing and financial support, staged a "boarding-home lunch". They served the mayor of Toronto and other officials the same food as that provided in the "facilities": watered down soup, cheap white bread, etc.. This was a short, small demonstration, but one that got a lot of attention.

h)   *Role Play.* Some, perhaps all, of the people may never have done anything this "public". They may have to be both trained and "psyched up", so that they can handle the excitement, the pressure, and the demand of the action. Also, this gets people into the habit of using other members' input. People can be asked to think up questions and share them with the group, and then have the group think up ways of dealing with them. Remember the demonstration belongs to everyone. They own it. You don't want anyone feeling used by the organization.

Demonstration Tactics

1.   Planning

As mentioned above, planning is important to the success of an action. There are a variety of areas that should be considered:

a)   Is there transportation needed to get people to and from the site?

b)   Is it at a time when most people can attend?

c)   Is the site familiar? Is it a large or small place?

d)   What numbers are appropriate?
- enough to get attention and impress the media, and/or opposition?
- not so many that it will be difficult for organizers to keep it going the way your people want it to?

e)   How long is it going to last?
- How long can your people "hang in"?
- Do some members need child care assistance?
- Are members clear on the time demands?
- Is there an estimate of how long the opposition can hold out?

f)   Who is in charge?
- Are there going to be marshals directing the members?
- How many marshals are necessary?

g)   Is everyone clear on the strategy and on what is expected of them?

h)   Is there a protocol for handling rowdies and hecklers? (see number 8 in this list)

i)   Are all the speakers lined up?
- How many?
- People belonging to the community organization? Sympathetic others?
- Is it clear what they will say?
- Is it clear how long they will take? Watch out for the well-intentioned long-winded person, or the guy on the ego trip.

j) Can we accommodate all the people who might wish to take part. For example, is there wheel chair access and/or translators for those with hearing and speech disabilities, etc.?

2. Is it the People's event?

The organizer should not be seen as a major force in the event. If somebody is to have her picture taken, or is asked for a quote, it should be a community member who:

- Is representative of the group;
- Is not the local egomaniac who will be seen as merely grabbing notoriety for herself.

> **Example:** It is not hard for an organizer to get caught in this. A community worker in Northern Ontario related how, at one of his group's first demonstrations against a school closing, he had been asked all the questions by the media present – the local paper and radio station. "It felt great being a media star at the time. I cringe now when I think how I took the spotlight away from the citizens who had a lot more at stake than I did".

3. Make sure that the focus of the demonstration is the appropriate one.

It is important to be clear as to who has the information or the decision-making authority in relation to the particular action contemplated. There is nothing more frustrating for a group than to have mobilized itself to march up to city hall or the legislature and be told that the relevant person is up or down one level. Obviously this can be a strategy that various levels of government play all the time - obfuscation of the issue, and buck-passing. Thus, it is important for the organization to have done its homework really well – make the opposition live up to their own rules as Alinsky advises – and be at the correct party's door with the correct demand.

4.   If it is a person you want to talk to, be sure he is there.

Again, it is very disconcerting to march to some official's office or house only to find he's at a conference in Sudbury. A ploy that is sometimes tried by the opposition is to set up a meeting where grievances will be aired or negotiations started. At the last minute, often as the meeting is to get underway, it is announced that the minister or director cannot be there, but that he has delegated so-and-so to sit in for him and that so-and-so will give him all the details later. A good general rule is that the organization should leave immediately, leaving the message that it is the minister or director whom we will talk to, or no one. While it is frustrating not to be able to "have your say", it is preferable to staying and wasting our time with some "flak catcher" who cannot (we can bet) give us anything but, "I'll be sure the ... sees your request and I am sure he will give it appropriate consideration". In effect we want to say: "We are important enough to deal with the top person – you are going to have to learn to treat us that way".

5.   Let other people know about the event.

There are a number of purposes for putting out sufficient word about our event:

a)   Some people may want to join the demonstration. We may wish to see them join, either to swell the numbers present, or to show the level and breadth of our support to the general community;

b)   There may be some important people who are straddling the fence on the issue for which the organization is fighting. It may be wise to keep these people informed on the objectives and scope of the action, rather than risking their getting a distorted view from either the media or the opposition. There is always, of course, a risk that some of the strategy may get "leaked", and this possibility must be weighed against the possibilities indicated above.

c)   There may be sympathetic people who wish to work behind the scenes on the issue, and for whom it is wise not to be at the scene of the event - so they are not forced to take a "public position";

Example: During a strike at a Children's Aid Society, there was one agency board member who, after some soul-searching and analysis, decided that management was manipulating the situation to prolong the strike and break the union. Her strategy became one of raising embarrassing questions with the Director and the agency bargaining team, and occasionally to leak board discussion to the union. Obviously, this person was invaluable to the workers and great care was taken to keep her informed of the time and place of any major demonstration, so that she could avoid potentially embarrassing situations and maintain her credibility with her co-board members.

6.   Invitations to "talk".

Occasionally, the people (or institution), against whom the demonstration is taking place will offer to talk things over with the demonstrators. It is a good idea to be prepared for this because, whether the intent is sincere or merely a ploy to cool down the event, it is an opportunity to escalate the pressure and to demonstrate the competence of the organization.

Sometimes the other side will invite a small number – the leaders – to go inside for a talk. It is important that the people decide:

a)   *Do we accept the invitation?* This is a question for the members to decide. Don't worry about making the other side wait – take some time to let our folks talk things over and make the decision.

b)   *How many people do we send?* It should not be everyone because the demonstration, or picketing, etc., must be maintained. On the other hand, it is important for the organization not to silently submit to the instruction of the opposition. The number chosen should reflect the needs and desires of the people, not those of the institution.

c)   *Who does the talking?* The other side, operating on their bureaucratic model, may want the leaders of the organization. The people, on the other hand, want to be consistent with the democratic nature of their organization. Besides this, the leaders of this public display may not be the organization leaders, and neither group may be the best suited to lead a delegation in this situation. Thus, it is important to have some sort of contingency plan on how to make these kinds of decisions, so that confusion does not occur and the appropriate decision can be made in good time.

d)   *Remember accountability.* If there is any chance that what may go on inside could lead to a decision that will affect the organization or the people demonstrating, the group that goes in **must** understand that they are accountable – that the decision is not final until the people say it is. It is a good idea to try to anticipate an offer so you don't get caught off-guard.

e)   *To whom will the delegation talk?* It is important for the group to clarify "what" is to be part of the discussion. As indicated above, it is frustrating and a waste of time to talk to a "flak catcher" who has no authority. Make sure that our people are going to be talking to decision makers.

7.   Use symbols

It is a good idea to use images that are symbolic of the principles, or cause, for which the community stands.

> **Examples:** A group of disability rights activists, in Cork, Ireland, wanted to draw attention to the many obstacles confronted by people with disabilities. A group with various disabilities - hearing, sight, etc. - pushed one of their wheelchair members all over the city. They videotaped themselves struggling with the wheelchair over curbs, and confronting inaccessible buildings. They presented the tape to a government Minister as support for their demand to have money spent on redressing the situation.

A wheelchair-bound activist - an example of using symbols to identify issues.

8.   Handling hecklers and rowdy bozos

One of the things that strikes fear into the hearts of many group leaders and organizers, is that a well-planned demonstration will be disrupted by people intent in turning things ugly – a brawl or a profanity-riddled shouting match, where the message gets lost in a hail of four letter words. If the potential for such a situation becomes apparent, we can consider the following:

a)   *Try accommodating the heckler.* Most hecklers thrive on situations where they are allowed to stand on the periphery of the crowd and yell inane comments and questions. It is important that the organization's speaker not get into a shouting or name calling match with them. It often can disconcert them to have a speaker offer them a few minutes "to have their say", or to ask their questions. They are not prepared for this – the strength of a heckler's position is his ability to play himself off what the speaker is saying – yet it is hard to refuse the offer. They have to come up and do the best they can or else they lose face. What they say is most often incoherent. Even if they are able to ask an embarrassing question, the speaker has gained time to think of how to deal with the issues the heckler has raised, as well as the sympathy of the audience. After being given the floor for a couple of minutes, it is difficult to go back to being a heckler. After all he's been given "his opportunity."

Note: If our people decide it is a good idea to heckle the opposition meeting, we must go armed with a prepared statement, or some facts and figures, in case the other side tries to pull this stratagem on us.

b) *Be firm with the rowdy.* Rowdies come in all shapes and sizes and with various motivations. They range from young fellows who have had too much to drink at the street dance, to a trained provocateur at a march on a picket line (Lakey, 1987) - witness the two undercover policemen carrying the banner at the April 1981 gay rights march in Toronto, and the ensuing violence. Both situations are tricky to deal with. Whatever one does, the general rule of thumb is to be prepared to handle the situation quickly.

- One method is to have a small group of marshals patrol the site of the event prepared to single out would be trouble makers. This method works best for keeping tabs on single people, particularly if it is a community person who is drunk or cranked up on drugs. The objective is to reduce the attention he is causing, and convince him to calm down or leave quietly.

Example: There is a wonderful scene in the 1939 film "Grapes of Wrath" in which a company goon squad tries to infiltrate the celebrations of a group of migrant farm workers in an attempt to start a riot, and discredit the people and their camp. Before they can foment anything, however, the thugs are quietly surrounded by a group of marshals who had been organized by the camp residents. The marshals escort them, firmly but peacefully, away from the celebrations.

- If things look at all like they might get out of hand, ask (or even demand) that the police handle it. If it is any kind of large event - particularly if it is a picket or a march - you know the police will be around. Do not let the situation get so out of hand that they will feel compelled to close the event down.

9.   Permits and Permissions

Any event that is going to use a public place – streets, a school yard or parking – is going to need some sort of authorization, perhaps a permit and maybe the co-operation of the police. Be sure someone in the organization is assigned to handle that.

Using the Media

Keep in mind, no matter how much "right wing" politicians and business people accuse the press of being "left wing", that the various print and electronic media are owned by people who are not in the least disadvantaged - Conrad Black's Holinger Corporation owns almost 50% of Canada's newspapers; Rupert Murdoch (the Australian gazillionaire) owns huge pieces of both print and electronic media around the world. The economic journalist, Linda McQuaig, tells a story of when she was working for the "Globe and Mail" (Canada's national newspaper):

She was asked to come into the managing editor's office to discuss a series she had been doing on the Canadian tax system. He warned her not to suggest that there was "some sort of class struggle out there". As Ms. McQuaig told her audience: "It was alright for there to be a class struggle, so long as we (the media) did not call attention to it". (McMaster University School of Social Work Field Forum, March 18, 1997).

There is no automatic belief in, or sympathy with, our cause - in fact it may be more reasonable to expect antipathy. Note the fact that, in 1998, David Black (owner of more than 60 newspapers in British Columbia) gave a directive to his journalists, that nothing in favour of the Nishga Treaty will be allowed in any of his newspapers' editorial sections - clearly an example of elites using the media to promote their own views and interests. Thus, it is unlikely we will ever get the kind of coverage we want. The welfare rights groups of the late 1960's were generally portrayed by the media as a gang of left-wing fanatics. The first social work strikes of the 1970's got very little print coverage at all. Later ones did not fair much better. Members of both "The

Right to Life" movement and "Abortion on Demand" groups complain that coverage is insufficiently sympathetic to their causes.

> **Example:** In Melbourne, Australia in 1991, a group of men held a rally and march to focus on male responsibility for violence against women. The event attracted over 300 participants; not bad for a first attempt. The major coverage came from a right wing columnist who ridiculed the purpose for, and the numbers of, the rally. For most of the rest of the media, it was treated as almost a non-event.

By and large, then, it would be unwise to depend on getting positive media coverage to further our group's interests. However, there are a few basic guidelines that should be kept in mind when planning a media event:

a)   *Be sure the various media know that an action is going to take place.* It is a good idea to have certain members try to develop contacts with particular media. However, even if this is accomplished, do not rely on that contact to be perfect and to always get our story right – the way we want it. The greatest benefit a contact can offer, especially on a newspaper, is his ability to let the organization know "the slant" the paper or station likes - so that we can tailor our communication with that in mind. We can also get a sense, from a good and honest contact, of how interested the particular medium is in the particular issue or cause represented by our organization. Finally, we can get a sense of "why" our great monster rally received no TV coverage, or only got four lines on the bottom of page 92 in the morning paper (just under the liver pill ad).

b)   *Keep the message clear and simple.* The more complicated the points we are trying to make with the public, the more likely the reporter or her editor will get something wrong. Be vigilant that our message does not get distorted by media that want a sensational story.

Example: "They did backflips for the attention of the media, but lost all control over the coverage when it came. On the rare occasions when reporters decided to do an 'East L.A.' story, they wrote up protestors and their targets Hollywood-style - as difficult warring 'personalities'. Or if they were especially sympathetic, they presented a sentimental victim scenario, utterly at odds with the IAF philosophy of competence and self-reliance". (Skerry, in Kerr 1993)

c)   *Make a TV event a TV event.* If the group wishes particularly to get some TV coverage then tailor that action for TV. (Watch political parties during election time). There are media events and there are mass rallies. The two often don't mix. A TV event should have something unique about it - a major announcement or some guerrilla theater; something that gives the station a reason for using it.

d)   *Be prepared to be innovative and take advantage of immediate conditions and situations.*

Example: Shannon Beard, a Canadian disability rights activist, tells the story of an initial information session held by the "Ontarians With Disabilities Act Committee" for Halton-Peel at the public library (stress on the "public"). This facility turned out to be most inaccessible for persons using wheelchairs, or with vision impairment. Though ramps were available for use, wheelchair users found them too narrow, and placed inappropriately. Very tight turns and a lack of space were a big problem. Persons with vision impairment had great difficulty, as the lighting was very dim, making reading material (and navigating one's way independently), very tricky. Ironically, this facility's barriers served to address the ODA's very core issues - lack of accessability. This proved beneficial when talking to the media and promoting ODA's goals. At a different time, some ODA committee members went to see an MPP in York region, and found the office inaccessible by wheelchair. Despite chilly winter conditions, the meeting was held in the parking lot, with local newspapers standing close by. A great media catcher, and a great statement to the community.

e)   *Designate a media liaison.* Have someone in the organization delegated to handle the media. He must be calm, and be able to handle himself in confusing circumstances.

f)   *Be careful not to get public media coverage before We are ready for it.* We want to utilize the media to get the message out, not simply to be used by them to sell papers or advertizing time. One danger is that the media coverage may raise expectations, and suggest that the issue is popular when it isn't (yet). It may raise expectations that something is going to happen quickly, when we know that rarely does any community development happen fast.

Also watch out! The press is pretty good at grabbing a member who is unprepared, and getting him to say something that sounds silly or inappropriate.

> **Example:** At a deputation, at a Hamilton City Council meeting by a local Native group, a couple of reporters were all over members of the group, asking if the members felt the remarks by some councillors had been racist. Everyone in the group referred them to one of three spokeswomen who were calm, prepared, and able to keep the tenor of the event "cool". It would have been good copy for the paper if racist charges had been leveled – and in fact one particular councillor had indeed angered the people with some paternalistic comments – but it had been planned by the organization, not as a media event, but as a low key education for councillors. There was no payoff for the group to start a controversy at that time.

g)   *Press conferences.*
  • Send out or fax a press package ten days before an event with: basic information; address; time; and any information you think they should have;
  • Repeat sending a press package the same the day of, and just prior to, the press conference;
  • Have an MC to: stop/start the conference; and to introduce those involved (make sure we know what they are going to say;
  • Target the particular press that we want. We will not want to bother with a station or paper that is likely to do a hatchet job on our organization or the issue;
  • Be there half an hour early, because the press will be there about then;
  • Have the press package with us, of up-to-date information that we want them to have. They will find it easier to report accurately, if they have this to use.

Technological Media[4]

One way of getting out information on our group, its events, or about issues in which we are interested and involved, is to use computer technology (O'Malley, 1998). This is an increasingly touted method of information exchange, keeping ourselves informed, keeping in touch, and for actual organizing. This can be a complex subject and one which we will only touch on briefly, but there are some clear reasons "why" we should consider the use of cyberspace:

1.   It can reach a lot of people very quickly;

2.   The message cannot be "interpreted" by an intermediary, who may not have the same values or point of view;

3.   It can foster debate, and bring in people who might not be reached in ordinary ways.

There are also some problems, associated with the use of cyberspace, that need to be recognized and considered:

1. Some folks (including this author) are a bit put-off by, or fearful of, complex technology for a variety of reasons;

2. Some folks will simply not have access to the technology either because of geography, or a lack of infrastructure (e.g.. a rural village in Africa or Latin America may not have electricity, let alone computers or software);

3. Some groups (here in North America and abroad) may not have the financial resources to purchase the basic technology required, or even some limited training to develop the skills needed to participate in such high-tech communication. In some sense, an uncritical espousal of high-tech information sharing can increase the distance between haves and have-nots. Some of this can be overcome by organizing those "with access" to support those "without ready access" - but this takes time, and we need to be clear on the payoffs for our group.

A Word About Civil Disobedience

Our discussion of demonstrations did not focus at any time on civil disobedience. This might seem strange, given the militant tone of much of this book and the urgency of many of the problems with which disadvantaged people are faced. The reason is not because such a discussion is unimportant. Indeed it is an important topic for an organizer, and requires consideration when the forces of a particularly odious status quo prove themselves to be totally unmoved by reasonable argument and legitimate protest. Mohandis Gandhi and his movements in South Africa and in India were forced to resort to civil disobedience. We note also some examples of civil disobedience in the civil rights activities, and Vietnam War protests of the 1960's and 70's. Today we see examples in the activities of First Nations People (attempting to bring resistant governments to the bargaining table over land claims and pollution issues) and in the actions of social justice groups confronting the neo-conservative agenda of the Ontario government. People who, after agonizing over an issue and deciding that as a last resort they must engage in an activity that risks arrest on a civil (not a criminal offence), must think through the implications both for themselves as individuals and for their organization (Amer, 1980: 115). (Some unions have been fined thousands of dollars for defying court orders.)

So, if civil disobedience is so important, why not deal with it at length? There are two reasons. First, as indicated above, civil disobedience is a serious and complex strategy undertaken as a last resort. A decision to engage in an endeavour of this kind requires sophisticated reflection and discussion. Defying a law - though a civil one, and even for very compelling reasons - is not something that is generally socially accepted in our society. When such a decision is made, it is necessary to spend time in planning and training. The law and its sanctions must be understood and training must be provided to ensure that none of the participants get injured, and so discipline is maintained. (Police can become frustrated, angry, and even frightened when faced with a large number of committed people). This book is primarily oriented to student organizers, or those relatively new to the field. It is not anticipated that these workers will be required to be involved in issues that call for the last resort of civil disobedience, at least not as organizers. As well, since most of the members of our society are not comfortable with the notion of "law breaking", and tend to equate it with violence, it is relatively unlikely that civil disobedience will occur as an option to very many groups. Secondly, there are some books available that treat the subject with sensitivity and creativity. *Yes We Can* (Amer, 1980: 15-20) and *Allow the Water* (Desroches, 1996) offer a Canadian perspective, and some interesting case examples. The three book series *The Politics of Non-Violent Action* (Sharpe, 1973), and Lakey's (1987) *Powerful Peacemaking* offer excellent material from an American perspective

Negotiation

In a contest situation, we expect that sooner or later (hopefully sooner) the organization is going to be invited to sit down by the opposition. It is going to be asked to make its case, and is going to be offered less than it demands. This is what happens when groups begin to negotiate.

Each side will begin with their "realistic ideal" position and over time will agree upon a realistic possible solution to the issue. The trick in negotiating is to have the final agreement closer to the people's "realistic ideal" than that of the opposition. It can be a long process, sometimes exciting but often tiring; and, as in every aspect of a community's striving to gain a measure of control over its own destiny, it takes diligent work and careful planning. Remember also that, ultimately, a deal is about redefining a continuing relationship in which the people will share power and resources.

1. Principles Guiding Negotiation

Never begin negotiating without:

a)   *A clear firm idea of what we need.* If we go in waffling, the other side will have every opening to waffle too. We are trying to change the other side; thus we have to be clear on what our situation is, and how we want it changed.

b)   *Helping the members be clear on what are the **analysis, values and principles** of what we are doing.* There will come a time for compromise, and it is these that will guide members in what we must have, what we can do without, and what can be altered.

c)   *A reasonably strong organizational base.* Remember, power - the ability to make something happen or not happen - depends on money, and/or information, and/or numbers of people. It is the latter that our organization has, as well as an issue. But having an issue that people are excited about is clearly not sufficient. Organization brings in people, and hopefully information; and thus, sometimes, expertise. This gives the people more power - without which, negotiation will never really take place.

d)   *Being clear on the context within which our group is negotiating.* This includes our own experience: be aware of our own personal style of using power and dealing with conflict. Obviously, we are not in a negotiating position because everything is smooth, everyone is in agreement and we can do what we want. Negotiation presupposes - even if at very low levels sometimes -

conflict and power. Thus, we need to be clear about our own personal tendencies, so that we can set that in the context of the principles that are at stake and the realities we face.

Example: On a personal note, my experience is that of a social worker and adult educator. I have worked as a union organizer, child welfare worker; with First Nations groups, neighborhood organizations, and housing co-operatives. I grew up in a poor neighbourhood, where we Irish Catholics fought Orange Protestants, and most kids didn't finish high school. I was unique in having a two-parent family. This has given me a particular slant on organizing, power, and the use of conflict. My initial tendency is to be abrasive and aggressive, and I need to be aware of that and moderate it, unless it is appropriate to the conditions and the needs and abilities of the people involved.

Some other questions to consider:

- What are the experiences of the people involved? (Be aware of areas where we may be weak in knowledge and experience, and work to strengthen them or minimize their impact).
- What does the opposition want? What are the opposition's strengths, and how do we deal with them?
- What is the history of the relationship with the opposition, and how might this effect the process?

e)   *Be clear on our own bottom line* - what we absolutely have to have. Again, be sure our people have thought this through.

2.   Tactics

a)   *Role play.* Never do any important negotiating without doing some role playing. Try to think of, and act out, the other side's feelings, tactics and responses. Practice our responses to these. Reduce surprise as much as possible.

b)   *Begin with a realistic but ideal position.* Do not start with our compromise position. Initially our group will "have to have" things we may be prepared to give up, but the other side should not see too soon what they are.

c)   *Don't send a leader to negotiate alone.* Use a delegation, a negotiation team. This gives the group an opportunity to broaden leadership and involvement. The team should be representative. There are three kinds of people for delegations:
   • those with a following;
   • those who work hard;
   • those who are able to take discipline.

d)   *Practice discipline.* While we should use a delegation, watch out for the other side's trying to pick us off one by one, or attempting to alter the focus of discussion – "Nice dress you have on there."; "Why is she so angry?"; "We don't have to be impolite." They will probably try to undercut our leadership, particularly if we are new at the game and they know it. Even though we can "smart-mouth" their people back, it can ruin our sense of order. Our leader should be the one to do the majority of the talking (see below).

   • One person should be in charge of the delegation to avoid confusion. This is the "spokesperson" or chief negotiator, not necessarily the leader of the organization. All comments should come from the spokesperson, unless our group has some planned operation; in that case the spokesperson should give the signal.

   • Use the spokesperson to run things through and keep things on track. If a member of our delegation has something to say, he should ask the spokesperson to ask it. Then the spokesperson can do what he wants with it. If their "chief" tries to deal with anyone else in our delegation, direct him back to our spokesperson. Usually that kind of discipline is unexpected by, and thus disconcerting to, the other side. We may want to use this tactic to keep control of an enthusiastic hot-head in our ranks, but at the same time train him in negotiation.

- If the spokesperson gets led off the agreed-upon track; or begins to go for a compromise too early, or something much less than is reasonable, ask for a caucus of our group. Ask their chief to take his delegation and leave the room. If he will not leave then say: "We'll go outside." Regardless of whether they cooperate, this tactic is usually disconcerting to the other side (outside their experience). It is always up to the chairperson to actually call, or to O.K., or delay the caucus if necessary. Don't caucus unnecessarily or repeatedly. That can make us look silly or unprepared. If there is a disagreement during the group's caucus, then we may have to use a disciplined majority vote (for speed in this kind of situation). The rules for "caucusing" must then be clear for everyone. (How to signal - always go through the leader, etc.). If someone breaks the rules she must be disciplined, **but** not in view of the other side. People **must** be prepared to call a caucus when they see the leader losing her way. At the same time, we have to be responsible and disciplined. As indicated above, we can't be yelling caucus every five minutes. The best rule is to get things as straight as we can before going into the meeting. It may be the organizer's role to move through the delegation encouraging or calming.

e) *Be clear about our own power.* Don't get into situations in which we have to produce but can't. This can hurt our group's credibility and morale.

f) *Define the rules of the negotiating meeting.* Keep pushing for our rules and be sure everyone is clear on them – where sessions are held; when it is most convenient for us and our people; whether the deliberations will be confidential; what items are on the table. (**Numbers** – we may want to bring more people than we agree to, unless the other side is on to this tactic, then bring less. Keep them off balance, if necessary).

Example: An instructive example of this tactic was related by a community worker in Northern Ontario. The area school board had decreed that in the interests of financial expediency, the local community school should be closed. This was a serious problem for the Native and White families of the area, as it meant that their children would have to be bussed many miles. After a lot of pressure they managed to get the Board to negotiate. A key session held at the community school itself. When the Board delegation arrived they found practically the whole community assembled. A Native leader had been elected chairperson, and sat at a table at the front of the hall. The Board people were allocated seats throughout the auditorium. It was a matter of "we talk you listen", with the power positions completely reversed. By the end of the meeting the closing decision had been completely reversed. While the tactic was not the only factor in the outcome, it did provide the community with an edge in confidence, and allowed them to push their position with as much force as possible.

g)   *Be careful about seating arrangements.*   Don't let one of the team become isolated. Be sure our people are in a position to easily communicate with each other.

h)   *Plan a mass action* – (If appropriate, see Demonstrations). Some people can go inside and negotiate and the rest stay outside to educate the public on the issues under negotiation. This makes the other side uncomfortable while grabbing publicity (or merely allows members to sing, dance, and enjoy themselves). The negotiating people inside must know who is outside. The mass action must be well choreographed. Plan ahead of time who is to go in, and who is to stay out. The people inside should be responsible to those on the outside – remember accountability. The negotiating team should report at the end of the proceedings, or in the middle if negotiating goes on very long. This action keeps the other side off balance while helping to solidify our group. Also, it is good modeling as an open, **evolving** people's organization.

i)   *Control the experts.* If experts (lawyers, accountants, architects) are used, they should "know their place" - i.e, under the control of the popular leadership. If, in an actual negotiating session, the organization has an expert to use, make sure the leader is still in control of our team. The experts work for the people. Do not let them jockey for position with those from the other side in a struggle that has nothing to do with why we are there. It is actually better to have the leadership extremely well schooled in the pertinent expertise, though sometimes it is also good to have a surprise (or mysterious) expert to keep the other side off balance. The important thing is teamwork, and having a captain who will pilot the action through.

Example: A group of workers, who were trying to negotiate their first contract, used a "mystery consultant". He was introduced simply as a "consultant" but nothing more. In actual fact he was helping the union do some organizing, and merely came along to observe. It turned out his presence knocked the management lawyer's concentration for a "loop". For the first two long sessions the lawyer would stare at him. Finally, near the end of the second session, the "consultant" asked for a caucus (because he thought the social workers' position was getting a bit confused). When the bargaining team came back in, the agency's lawyer stood up triumphantly and yelled, "Ah ha, I knew it all the time, you're their labour relations expert". The group burst out laughing. Nobody said anything, but you could feel the team's confidence rise as they perceived the other side confused and off-balance.

j)   *Look for common principles and practical common ground.* Our group may have a number of issues it wants resolved. Some will be easier than others because they do not challenge the power of the other side. It is helpful to look for commonalities because:
  • It gives everyone on both sides a sense of accomplishment;
  • It sets a constructive tone;
  • If they are left to the end of a tough continuous set of negotiations, they may turn into hard issues.

Help the other side see where its self-interest is enhanced by our position, or at least where it is not harmed.

k)   *Do sufficient research on the other side (this may cost money).* Understand where their "bottom line" really is. It is important for us to be able to recognize when there is some real movement, or compromise, on their part. It is no use trying to push them farther than they can legitimately go, or further than our people need. On the other hand, we don't want to be fooled into accepting a supposedly magnanimous offer when the other side can afford to give more.

l)   *Use of third parties.* If things get tough, don't be afraid to slow down the process. We may want to see if we can get other people involved as mediators (formally, informally or even secretly). Remember our "neutral" group from earlier in the chapter. This may be a good place to look for a mediator.

> **Example:** A group of First Nations people were involved in a struggle with the administration of a Native Centre. They felt (not without reason) that the director had not been managing the Centre in the interests of the whole community. The director had supporters - mostly on the board of directors. After months of bitter negotiations about what should be done, the two sides were so far apart that they could not even meet. The citizen group called on a non-Native professor at the local university. He was sympathetic to them, but not directly involved. He got the parties back to the table.

m)   *Get the other side to put its points in writing.* If there is some agreement, get them to specify the actions to be taken, any steps involved, and the timelines.

n)   *If we decide to compromise, be sure to make it clear to the "other" that we have given up some of our position.* In this way we are doing two things:
   • Modelling unselfish behaviour;
   • Gaining a moral high ground.

By the way, if the "other" does some compromising of signifi-
cance, we have to be prepared to acknowledge that and consider
what this means to our position. (Be aware, however, of the
"yellow carnation".)

o)   *Be prepared that in some cases there may be irreconcilable differences.* This is rare. Nevertheless, it is not useful to keep negotiating, no matter how much we want to come to an agreement, if we are being jerked around. Sometimes, for our sanity
or reputation, we have to walk away from negotiation and either
seek more adversarial strategies or abandon the issue.

Reflection

Popular action is the key to positive change. It involves citizens doing
what they believe needs to be done, on issues that they have chosen
and understood as important to their lives. It is not always about winning
- not that this is not important. In popular action we are not only trying
to achieve concrete results; we are also learning from our reflections
on our actions - learning about ourselves, our adversaries, and the issues
themselves. Popular action is also not only limited to strategies and
tactics - though or course they are important in taking strong, positive
action. It is worth repeating Freire here - activity without reflection is
simply activism. Part of what we want to achieve is an increase in the
people's (and our own) understanding of the world in which we act.

Endnotes

[1] By 1996 Diashowa had experienced so much damage from the strategy that
it attempted to smash it by applying for a court injunction against the actions
of the Friends. While a court provided the injunction, in 1998 the petition was
denied by a higher one on the obvious grounds that the company was attempting
to suppress free speech.

[2] See Richard Wagamese (1996) *That Terrible Summer;* and the film by
Alanais Obonsowin, "Kanehsatake 270 Years of Resistance" for excellent
documentation.

³   Many of struggles entered into by these people necessitated the use of civil disobedience. (See "An Historical Perspective" in Introduction).

⁴   For a good discussion of the use of high-tech communication, see Kady O'Malley's, *"Grassroots in Cyberspace"*; or Rykert and James (1998), *Working Together On-Line.*

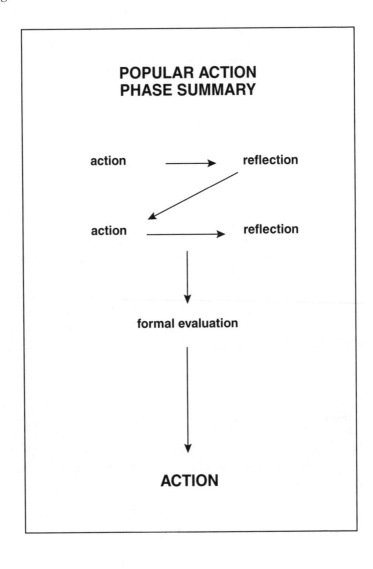

Chapter

Chapter

9

EVALUATION

The unexamined life is not worth living.

—*Socrates*

Evaluation is important to community organizing for one obvious and important reason: it is one method by which the accountability of the organizer to her funding organization and/or group is exercised. In one aspect, evaluation seeks to discover the degree to which the community organizer was able to actualize the goals and objectives of the funding body. However, this should not be the sole purpose; it is rare that a sponsor can specify objectives that are sufficiently concrete and measurable. As well, when the funder is a secondary or outside entity, it is not in a strategic (or moral) position to develop objectives that are sure to be relevant to community members. Finally, we have spoken already (see Chapter 5) of the process of transferring accountability for what the organizer does from the funder to the community itself. So, as well as relating to the goals and objectives of the sponsor; the community's goals, objectives and strategies must be taken into consideration. For example, does the community now have better resources, more power or better participation?

While these are good questions in general, they are just that - general. They don't really direct us to think about whether the objectives are realistic, for example; or how widespread within the community is the power that has been achieved; or how anything was accomplished. A comprehensive evaluation will ask both descriptive questions (such as "what happened?") and analytical ones (such as "how did things happen?" and "why did they happen the way they did?"; or "how were people involved and why?").

As well as the "informing" questions that need to be asked for a thorough evaluation, there are some principles that are useful to keep in mind throughout this process.

Principles Guiding Evaluations

1.   *Early and explicit inclusion of evaluation process.* As stated earlier, evaluation is most helpful and most possible if it has been built into the organizing process at the outset. This does not mean that we've had to arrange for a set of "before and after question-naires" and a computer program. It does mean that the "fact" of evaluation, and reality that the funder will indeed want a report, should be made clear as soon as possible. It should also be clear "why" the evaluation is to be done, and what implications it has:

     • End or scaling down of the project or community worker time?
     • Refunding?
     • A new role for the worker?
     • A new direction for the project?
     • Anything else?

2.   *Community awareness and involvement.* The people in the com-munity must be aware that it's occurring. Further, they should be involved in a central way. After all this evaluation is bound to have some effect on them; and, given our stance that the com-munity should be able to affect their environment and their lives, this should be somewhat under their control.

     • The process of developing the evaluation generally should be an open one, with the opportunity to give input available to as many members as possible. (Remember the community analysis). Thus, it is important to be clear about who gets to frame the questions, and why.

• Similarly, it is important to make sure there is widespread opportunity for people to have their opinions heard. There is also the issue of form and language. The report must be useful to the membership - not simply a bureaucratic or academic exercise that will gather dust on someone's shelf.

• The findings should be available to everyone. One of the frustrating things that funders sometime do is evaluate programs or agencies and then sit on the results.

Example: A team of community workers were contracted to provide an evaluation of a small but very active Northern Ontario community. Both the organization and the evaluation were funded by a government ministry. The evaluation showed that the organization was well known and well thought of in the community. The report was sent in to the ministry, but after a couple of months it had not been released to the community or made public in any way. This seemed strange as the ministry officials had been very insistent that it be done. After a lot of insistence by the organization and the consultants, the report was finally released at a meeting among the organization, ministry officials and the consultants. The officials were highly critical of the report, and claimed the findings were not useful. Later, however, at a private meeting with the consultant, the official said that he hoped that there were no hard feelings. He noted that the report really wasn't that flawed, and said, "The problem is simply that you wrote the wrong report. We wanted ammunition to end funding for this project. We didn't want good news. We thought you'd understand."

3. *There should be very few surprises.* Because the process is "built in", and as it is a "public" one, the members the community should be prepared for both the questions and findings. Of course, there

will be nuances, but there should not be anything that comes out of left field.

4. *Be clear about who gets to frame the question and who does not.* This is very important. Whose perspectives are going to be presented?

Questions Concerning the "Content" of Evaluation

The questions that are developed are going to be more specific and oriented to concrete community situations (remember our objectives in Chapter 2) than these below, but these are the types of questions that should be asked.

1.   The Community

a)   Did the community develop some degree of influence relative to its needs, its environment or its problems?

b)   How is success to be measured?
  • In its relationship with the broader community? Is it seen more positively? Does it have more influence?
  • By the degree to which identified problems have been solved?
  • By the presence or absence of necessary new or improved resources in, or available to, the community (members)?
  • By the degree of participation of members in the community?
    - Is the participation meaningful? Does it have an effect?
    - Is it around minor issues or major ones? Why?
    - Is the participation varied? (i.e., are some types of issues or events more "popular" than others; or are some areas of the community more active than others?)
  • By the change in degree or nature of conflict within the community? Is there more conflict or less conflict within the community? Just as important, is conflict dealt with in a healthy constructive manner?

- By the change in communication patterns within the community? How would people see the quality of communication among themselves, and between themselves and the community organization?
- By the number and quality (effectiveness and accessability) of grassroots organizations?
- By the change in the breadth of leadership within the community? Has there been a proliferation of leadership roles?
- By the extent to which the leadership has been effective? And how?
- By the knowledge and skill level of members?
- In the extent to which the community has developed a better analysis (or picture) of itself and the conditions its members face?
- By an increase in pride of membership - in the way people see themselves; their knowledge, culture, and traditions?

2.   Programs and activities

a)   Which strategies have been successful and which have not? How is this success to be measured:
- By the numbers involved?
- By the degree of consumer satisfaction?
- Through the measurement of some sort of behavioral change? (Such as less vandalism or drug use, or more visiting among members).

b)   Were the programs and activities consistent with the goals and objectives of the community? This is not a pejorative question. If inconsistencies are present it may merely mean that the original goal and objectives were not "right", or that the process that developed them was lacking in some way.

c)   Were there unforeseen results - positive or negative - from any of the programs or activities?

d)   Were there any changes in objectives at any time?
- When did they occur?
- Under what circumstances?
- What process of change was used?

e)   Are present directions clear? Do people know what they, as a community, wish to accomplish; or are they waiting around for someone to give them the word?

3.   Opposition

a)   Who turned out to be the opposition?
      • within the community.
      • external to the community.

b)   Under what conditions did opposition arise?

c)   Relative to what issues was there opposition?

d)   How effective was the opposition?

e)   How effective was the community in countering it?

f)   Were we able to swing people from opposition to neutrality, or even further?

4.   Allies (outside of the community members)

a)   What individuals or institutions turned out to be helpful?

b)   Under what conditions did allies surface?

c)   Relative to what issues were allies available?

d)   How effective were the allies?

e)   Did we maintain the support of our original supporters?

5.   The Organizer

Clearly many of the questions outlined above reflect on the organizer. In some ways the organizer can take some credit or blame in that he has initiated and facilitated many of the processes that have shaped the present circumstance of the community. However, some specific questions that get at organizer effectiveness are:

a)   Can the activities run without him? Why or why not?

b)   Has an unapproachable elite been formed within the community?

c)   Have internal divisions been cleared or exacerbated?

d)   Are internal divisions being handled in a better way?

e)   Do members see him realistically (e.g., as a facilitator or initia-
      tor) or unrealistically (e.g., a saviour or a devil)? Are members
      able to see the part, or role, that the organizer has played in their
      growing sense of themselves, and growing sense of responsibil-
      ity and power over their own lives?

Reflection

Sometimes it is more appropriate for a community to undertake a review
of its activities rather than an evaluation. The differences between the
two are important. An evaluation suggests that the project will be
investigated and judged according to some set of objective criteria.
Emphasis is placed primarily on outcomes. A review, on the other
hand, seeks to understand the work that the group is doing in a critical
manner - the issues it is dealing with, and the context within which it
exists. This reflects the fact that people grow and change. Often, in
community work, it is difficult to arrive at so-called objective
(unchanging) criteria on which to make judgements. The context is
highly complex and the work is fluid - responding to local and
surrounding changes. A review can be critical, useful in posing and
answering questions, but it can also be useful in mobilizing thought
and support for progressive change among those who participate.
Remember the thoughts of McGrath (1998): "Critical investigation helps
people to look at social problems in the light of what they wish to
achieve as self-reliant and self-determining social beings".

All this is not to suggest that evaluations are not useful - indeed they
are often required - but rather that it is wise to strive for the spirit of a
review. Its breadth and fluidity offer us a way to focus outcomes,
context, and process as dynamic, interrelated parts of a puzzle - one
that is never quite solved, but becomes more interesting and intelligible
the more we examine the pieces in various combinations.

Chapter

10

THE END

We shall not cease from exploration.
And the end of all our exploring, will be to
arrive where we started.
And know the place for the first time.
                    —*T.S. Elliot (*from The Four Quartets*)*

Sooner or later the organizer is going to be pulling up stakes and leaving the community. Ideally this should happen when she has "worked her way out of a job", and the community no longer needs her. However, there are many reasons for separation from the community when there is still work to be done.

Reasons for Leaving a Job Early

1.   Worker Fatigue

We become tired from meeting the demands of a very challenging job. We may need to take time off, or may need a fresh experience.

Worker fatigue or burnout is an all too common occurrence in all forms of social helping or solidarity work. Lakey et al. (1995), Shields (1994), Cruikshank (1989) and Burghardt (1982) all point to how hard and frustrating the work is; and how it can effect us in negative ways. They suggest various ways of managing and/or overcoming it. Three simple approaches are outlined below:

- Be reflective - Take time to think about how we are reacting to people and situations.
    - How much of it is the situation? Sometimes it is just plain chaotic and crazy.
    - How much of it is the people with whom we are working? They too get tired, or caught up in their own unresolved issues.
- Get or stay connected - Don't try to be a "Lone Ranger". We need to find people we can trust, and with whom we can build supportive relationships. Others can also help us reflect.
- Take a break - If we are not operating effectively we may need to rest a bit. While the pace may be hectic, we can only put off taking care of ourselves for a limited time.

2. Need for New or Different Skills

Difficult though this is to face for most of us, we are not masters of all trades. A developing community may have continuing need for an organizer, but one with different skills than the ones we possess. This can be difficult for both the organizer and the community to deal with; after all, organizing is a personal as well as a political endeavour. Particular relationships will become highly valued and will cause some pain to break off. However, staying beyond one's time can be injurious to both the community and the organizer.

3. The Funding Dries Up

There are times when, through no fault of anyone in the community, a project loses its funding. This can happen when, for example, government is elected or a new administration enters the picture. It can be relatively sudden; and even when it is not, the pain of seeing long term work go for nothing can be disheartening. In this case, it is important for people to come together to understand that it is not the fault of the community, and to celebrate some of the good things that have taken place along the way. As well, it is important to allow participants to voice their feelings of anger, frustration or betrayal. This also needs to be a time for support and analysis - a time to be shared among activists.

> **Example:** In Ontario, when the right-wing conservative government took office, it all but scrapped its Housing Advocacy Program. Many good projects were cancelled, among them the Affordable Housing Action Association of Mississauga. At one of the last meetings, a number of people spoke of the disappointment and feelings of defeat. A couple of participants, however, stated that while they had worked hard, and had hoped for long term success, they had seen enough of life to realize that the group had been engaged in something that would require a long battle against some powerful elites, and one where many losses could occur. They pointed to some of the small successes that the group had, and maintained that they were disappointed but not defeated - they would continue to look for opportunities to involve themselves in good projects. People started to build on this, and the gloom began to lift. This helped the group see itself in a more positive (but not unrealistic) light, and helped to maintain a level of hope for the future. It helped turn what could have been a defeated, disempowered group of people into one that saw itself as part of a long term struggle.

4. The Organizer Becomes a Target

As has been noted all through this book, community work is hard. It's hard for the workers, and for the people with whom we work. Previous discussions that noted they may have undergone lengthy, serious, and damaging situations which makes it difficult for them to act in the most logical or long term manner. (Remember the notion of frustration instigated behaviour). Almost all community workers can relate stories of really good people, workers and activists who ran into trouble as a result of internal community or organizational politics.

Every so often a community worker does make a serious mistake. One situation that can force a person out occurs when serious division arises in the community between two equally strong factions. The organizer may feel she has to take one side or the other – perhaps because she feels one side is totally wrong, or is being very destructive. In this kind of situation the organizer herself can sometimes become the issue (i.e., a target for the internal hostility). It can become like a civil war and, as we know, these are the most vicious and dirty of all conflicts. Again, it can be a hard thing to face; but if she feels that she is becoming the issue, or is becoming personally consumed by it, then it is time that she seriously considers leaving. Clearly this is a very difficult issue and she should seek some outside consultation before she makes up her mind to do anything drastic.

> **Example:** A white community worker was involved in some volunteer work in a Native community. A small but powerful group (including another white person) attempted to seize control of an important Native agency in the city. Part of their strategy was to accuse the worker of "manipulating" the agency and people. After consultation with some community members it was decided that he should withdraw from the conflict and the community. In his absence the issues were relatively easy to clarify, and the power grab became obvious. With time the community was able to resolve the issues creatively. The other white person who had chosen to stay in the conflict had to leave the community and the volunteer worker was invited to return. His credibility was stronger, and the community itself had gained confidence by handling a difficult situation themselves.

5.   The Organizer Gets Another Job

It is quite possible that a good organizer may receive a number of job offers in the course of working with her community. An offer may be made that she "cannot refuse". (On the other hand, we need to be careful that we don't move from a job too soon). A good community worker will become well known, and attractive job offers may come after only a short time with a community. The opportunities of the new position must be weighed against any possible damage to one's reputation or to the community. It is not a sign of failure for the community to need a worker to follow us.

> **Note:** It is important to realize that, while we may need to move on, that community may still require assistance. Don't get caught in the myth that unless we have worked our way out of a job we are failures. Given the difficulties that communities face, that may be unrealistic in the time we have had together. As one thoughtful community worker once said, "Most of the communities we work with have so much against them that it may take years and years of hard work before they won't need a worker to follow us anymore".

The Leave-Taking

1.   Negative Possibilities

Whatever the reason for the termination, it is a crucial event for the organizer and her community. It is not uncommon for people to feel abandoned, hurt, or even angry, no matter how long they have known about the departure. There may be some fear that "we can't make it without you". Though, in fact, the members may well be able to stand on their own feet, and may have been doing so for a while, it is still frightening to have to do things without the familiar backup of the community organizer.

a)   *Community members may act negatively toward the organizer -* people can make an organizer "pay" for abandonment. This may take the form of:
   • guilt trips;
   • displaced anger – sometimes an organizer who is leaving can become the target of anger that is really aimed at other organizations or community members. The organizer can be blamed for work being incomplete;
   • unrealistic last minute demands;

   Example: An organizer in a housing co-operative had two weeks to go before she left her position. At that point, one of the members of the board of directors suggested that she mount and complete a survey of the 125 or so member families in the project. Needless to say the organizer had only sufficient time to explain why she could not take on that big a job in that short a time.

   • unreasonable rejection of the organizer's ideas.

b)   *Organizer may act negatively toward the community.* It is possible too for the organizer to feel guilty and vulnerable. If she is not clear on her feelings she can inadvertently do some destructive things like:
   • leaving with very short notice, and leaving the people with the feeling that they have been abandoned;
   • making unrealistic last minute demands on members;

   Example: A community worker, with a subsidized housing group, attempted to get his members to purchase some leadership training from some consultants about three weeks before he was to leave. When he felt that they were not moving so that the contract would be in place before he left, he got angry and berated the president of the association in front of the executive and the consultants. The president was embarrassed and confused, and the consultants embarrassed. They had to spend some time dealing with the

damage done to the president's confidence. The worker had
been concerned that he leave no loose ends. However, his
anxiety got in the way of good sense, and he actually hurt his
own purpose.

- volunteering to do a bunch of tasks for which he or she has
  little or no time;
- projecting an "I don't care" image;
- suggesting or taking on new projects that mean something to
  him, but for which the community organization is not ready;
- etc.; the possibilities are many.

2.   Positive Possibilities

Having laid out the potential for difficulty we should stress that it need
not be a doom, defeat and despair situation. The reverse can in fact be
the case. People can see the departure as an indication that important
work has been accomplished. The departure of one organizer can be a
catalyst for the community to look at itself, its objectives, and its tactics
– this can either be within the framework of evaluation (review chapters
7 and/or 9) or outside of it, if necessity dictates. Finally, it can be a
time for the organizer to receive a few positive personal strokes.

3.   To Ensure the Best Results

a)   The majority of our relationships are, in some ways, transitory.
       At some time, every relationship but the most brief involves feel-
       ings, and often their passing involves victories as well as losses.
       We should be able to talk about each, i.e., it is important that we
       model the appropriate handling of termination – acknowledge
       feelings (ours and theirs).

b)   Make sure the community has sufficient lead time - two weeks is
       not enough; six months may be too long. This is not to suggest
       you should keep things secret. However, if something appears
       to be too far in the future people may just ignore it; so the organ-
       izer has to be prepared to remind people ten to twelve weeks in
       advance.

c) Be prepared for negative feelings and actions. They may not be too overt; you may have to do a little verbalizing for folks to get their feelings into the open, or so they will free themselves to talk about them.

d) Don't wait too long for people to raise the question of your departure. This may be the first time you have had to initiate something for some time. There is nothing wrong with initiating discussion now if the people aren't up to doing it themselves.

e) Be clear about why you are leaving. Of course, it may be obvious; but if it is not, be declarative. Any attempt to soft peddle or avoid tough issues may lead to rumours and distrust - this can drain community energy from necessary tasks and objectives.

f) Be clear about how we feel about leaving. This helps your members do the same – good modelling is as important at the end as at the beginning.

   Example: A worker in a small Northern Ontario community related that, after overcoming some fears of how an announcement would be treated, he found people more open and direct with him than ever before. They even began to joke with him, "over-verbalizing" not only their own feelings, but his own. His leaving, or rather the way in which he handled it, probably liberated some feelings and energy to deal with important issues facing the entire community.

g) Be sure to tie up any loose ends as much as humanly possible. Whether someone is following us or the members are on their own, it is neither fair nor good practice to have others finishing things that we could have handled.

h) Affirm realistically that people can do what they need to do. We may need to point out how much they have achieved.

i) Clarify our future role:
   • don't undercut the next worker;
   • don't set up false expectations;
   • don't dismiss the feelings of members. They are real and need attending to.

j)   If a new community worker is to be following us, get it clear as
       to if and how we will be involved in the replacement process.
       Will we be involved through:
       • being on the hiring committee;
       • developing a job description;
       • ad hoc consultation.

Don't Forget to Celebrate

However we have come to the end of the journey, we owe it to ourselves
to have a bit of a celebration. We may not (likely have not) won
everything that we wanted. On the other hand, unless things have gone
seriously awry, something has been gained. We need to look at our
accomplishments with the people we have been working with, and
celebrate them. Moyer (1990) and Burghardt (1982) have pointed out
that community workers sometimes miss the opportunities to celebrate
the big as well as the small successes. As we end our association with
our group, we should not let the opportunity pass.

Members of Banamwandu Project in Uganda celebrate their successes.

Reflection

Leaving a community may be every bit as difficult as entering it, though the dynamics are clearly quite different. In any event both entry and exit demand creativity and courage. In both instances there is an understandable temptation to "do it quickly", or to "run away". In both instances the pay-off comes in being careful, complete, direct, and clear in: our communication; our purposes; and caring for the people we've worked with. As in the beginning we had to give the citizens the opportunity to use us, in the end they need to have the opportunity to let us go.

AFTERWORD

Community Work:
An Unfinished Practice

In the first section of this book we briefly outlined the work of a number of activists who had been successful in bringing people together and assisting them to alter significant aspects of their lives. We then looked at the inequalities that so many people face, and why they need to organize themselves. Third, we examined the specific goals and objectives of community development work. Finally, we briefly examined key roles and skills in community practice. For the majority of the book we explored the issues and tasks that workers face in attempting to reach their objectives. As we end it is worthwhile to describe three admonitions that reflect some of the contradictions or unfinished aspects of community organization.

Earlier there was a plea to think about the phases of community work as interweaving, not totally discrete phases. While we might be emphasizing one more than another at any particular time, development requires attention to all of them. As neither the phases nor the objectives are separate among themselves, so the phases and objectives cannot be seen as separate from each other. They have been described in separate sections but will be pursued and practiced together. Though there is no road map to guide us in precisely the right direction, it is the challenge of each community worker to think about them as deeply coherent.

A second admonition is to reiterate that we need to be very clear about the broader context of our work. We noted the pervasiveness of inequality and the importance, particularly, of class issues. These class issues are becoming more marked as globalization and concentration of capital are becoming stronger. Often we respond (need to respond) defensively, trying to hang on to what security disadvantaged communities have gained in the past. Of course this is something that is important. On the other hand, however, we need to take a more proactive stance. In this vein it might be useful to pose a couple of rather broad questions. They are by no means the only questions that can and should be asked about context. Rather, they are examples that suggest the linkage between the broad issues of values and policy, and the specific questions of community development practice.

Why haven't the values of capitalism worked? Since the fall of totalitarian communism in Eastern Europe, there is a great tendency to ask questions about why socialism didn't work. Leaving aside the argument as to whether socialism ever really existed there, we need to focus people on the real failures of the values of western capitalism - unequal growth, competition, bureaucracy, elitism. Have they eradicated racism, sexism, poverty? Indeed, have they not contributed to their perseverance? Many of the values of community work (collective action, egalitarianism, co-operation) are linked to those of socialism. In focusing on "why" socialism has failed, we are really asking why these values have failed. Rather, a more useful activity is (surely) to challenge the values of capitalism, to alter the ground of the debate. In this way we can perhaps stimulate a more productive discourse, and the values underlying a developmental approach can be honestly explored.

Why doesn't bureaucracy work? As we mentioned in Chapter 1, it is held to be the efficient way to run any group's affairs. The fact is, however, that as well as alienating individuals from their work, bureaucratic conglomerates (newly downsized and well equipped with the latest technology) all over the world have failed miserably in the goal that they care the most about - making money efficiently. The

Savings and Loan fiasco in the U.S.A. cost billions of dollars. Asian markets have crumbled in the mid 90's. In Canada, the major banks make obscene profits while denying loans to small business people, and nickel and diming customers with irritating service charges. We have every right to ask whether technological bureaucracy, is at all suitable for modern society; let alone for community groups. And if bureaucracy is inappropriate, can we liberate ourselves for a serious search for forms that will be both efficient and effective?

Allied to the question of bureaucracy, is that of size. The number and size of amalgamations is taking place at record pace. But, again, has this added to the quality of life of humanity? Income disparity between the rich and the poor nations increases, as well as between rich and poor classes in the developed world. If anything, great lumbering organizations seem to cause more misery than progress. As Lewis Lapham (1998) has so aptly put it: "The concentrations of wealth work against the concentration of the mind. People accustomed to buying things instead of making things often substitute size for the lack of a better idea, or any idea at all". We have every right and responsibility to ask then, how does "bigness" work for people? Clearly, the trend takes us further from community and more toward bureaucratic standardization. In whose interest is this being managed?

Interestingly, as business interests celebrate the elephantine proportions of its empires, we are seeing the attack on the welfare state. Why? With all its over-centralized notions of planning and bureaucratic rigidity, it allowed for the most caring and just social arrangements in the history of western industrialized society. Why are we being urged to "go back" to a society that was based on individual competition, and away from compassion and shared responsibility? It was the failure of market mechanisms to deal with the ravages of unfettered capitalism that led us to look for collective solutions to human problems. In whose interest are we being sold a vision of a return to the 19th century?

These questions are important, and they are posed not as part of some academic exercise. They have practical implications for us and for the people we help organize. Community development is deeply concerned with social institutions and organization. They reflect the underlying social, economic, and political attitudes of society. They are the mediating structures that shape the relationships that express our empowerment or disempowerment. It is in this sense - of holding a critical stance toward the dominant ideas and institutions - that our practice should never be finished. Of course, community workers need to continually hone intervention skills – communication, analysis, strategy, etc.. We must also be constantly prepared to reflect critically on where our society is; where our institutions are leading us; how our practice is being influenced; and how we are influencing others to either accept, or challenge, the status quo.

A bit of unfinished business relates to an irony in community work practice. Though community development is a collective endeavour, the person hired to do the organizing is more often than not an outsider - a person not of the community. We are not members of the community who will always live in the communities in which we work. We are not leaders who can draw strength from the energy that people give to them. We are, no matter how much we identify with a people's struggle, outsiders. This has the advantage that our position can provide us with a unique perspective and opportunities for learning. While there is no doubt that our liberation is intimately bound to that of the people, and though we can share in their victories and defeats - in the final analysis these victories and defeats are uniquely theirs. We must not create some romantic notion that because we believe and live in a struggle that we somehow mystically become the same as the oppressed. We must come to terms with that. As such, community work can often be quite lonely. Some link community worker burnout to this dynamic. It is difficult to find someone with whom to share the unique experience of being an organizer. It is quite important, then, to look for colleagues with whom to share experiences. In doing the research on community work objectives, it was not uncommon to hear someone say; "You know, I never get to talk about stuff like this. I know I need to. It clears my head. But it's hard to find people who know what I'm feeling or talking about." We need to make the effort to establish connections among ourselves – to challenge and support each other, and to assist in the work of thinking critically about the work of community organizing.

Community work is something that, like society itself, is always growing and changing. We as practitioners need to see it as something hopeful.

Let no one be discouraged by the belief there is nothing one man or woman can do against the enormous array of the world's ills - against misery and ignorance, injustice and violence...few will have the greatness to bend history itself; but each of us can work to change a small portion of events, and in the total of all those acts will be written the history of this generation.

It is from the numberless diverse acts of courage and belief that human history is shaped. Each time a person stands up for an ideal, or strikes out against injustice, or acts to improve the lot of others, he sends a tiny ripple of hope, and crossing each other from a million different centres of energy and daring, those ripples build a current which can sweep down the mightiest walls of oppression and resistance.

—Robert Kennedy

BIBLIOGRAPHY

Abrams, C. et al. 1994. *A Manual for Social Development Practice (2nd ed.).* Columbo: National Institute of Social Development.

Adams, I. 1970. *The Poverty Wall.* Toronto: McClelland and Stewart Ltd..

Adamson, N. et al. 1988. *Feminist Organizing for Change.* Toronto: Oxford University Press.

Albert, J. 1992. *If we don't do it who will?* Vol. 23 pp. 665-684. Canadian Social Work Review.

Alinsky, S. 1971. *Rules for Radicals.* New York: Random House.

Amer, E. 1980. *Yes We Can.* Ottawa: Synergistics Consulting Limited.

Amnesty International Bulletin. The breaking of minds and bodies: The long journey home. December 1989/January 1990. Vol.XVII:no.1 (pp. 10-13).

Antone, R. et al. 1986. *The Power Within People.* Deseronto, Ontario: Peace Tree Technologies.

Arnstein, S. 1969. Eight rungs on the ladder of citizen participation. *Journal of the American Institute of Planners. 3:4.*

Atkinson, D. and L. Elliott. 1998. Anxious? Insecure? You'll get used to it. *Guardian Weekly.* June 21:pp.1-4.

Ball, R.A. 1973. The analgesic sub-culture of the southern Appalachians. In I.A. Spergle (ed.), *Community Organization: Studies in Constraints.* Beverly Hills: Sage.

Bandura, A. 1978. The self system in reciprocal determinism. *American Psychologist.* April:344-358.

Barker, R.L. 1991. *Social Work Dictionary (2nd. ed.).* Silver Springs, MD: NASW Press.

Barndt, D. and C. Freire. 1989. *Naming the Moment (monograph).* Toronto: Jesuit Centre for Faith and Justice.

Barnesley, J. and D. Ellis. 1992. *Research for Change.* Vancouver: The Women's Research Centre.

Berton, P. 1980. *The Invasion of Canada.* Toronto: McClelland and Stewart.

Biddle, Wm. and L. Biddle. 1965. *The Community Development Process.* New York: Rinehart and Winston.

Biklen, D.P. 1983. *Community Organizing Theory and Practice.* Englewood Cliffs, New Jersey: Prentice-Hall Inc..

Bishop, A. 1994. *Becoming an Ally: Breaking the Cycle of Oppression.* Halifax: Fernwood Publishing.

Bloomberger, W. Jr. 1969. Community organization. In R.M. Kramer and H. Specht (eds.), *Readings in Community Organization Practice.* pp. 91-127. Englewood Cliffs, New Jersey: Prentice-Hall.

Boff, L. 1982. *St. Francis - A Model for Human Liberation.* New York: Crossroads Publishing Company.

Booth, H. 1974. *Handbook for Organizing Women.* Chicago: Midwest Academy.

Boothroyd, P. 1991. Community development: The missing link in welfare policy. In B. Kerwin (ed.), *Ideology, Development and Social Welfare: Canadian Perspectives.* Toronto: Canadian Scholars Press.

Bowles, S. and H. Gintis. 1976. *Schooling in Capitalist America.* New York: Columbia University Press.

Bregha, F.J. 1971. Community development in Canada: Problems and strategies. In J. Draper (ed), *Citizen Participation in Canada.* pp. 72-83. Toronto: New Press.

Breshlow, Ruban L. 1976. *Worlds of Pain.* New York: Basic Books Inc.

Brown, J.M. 1989. *Gandhi: Prisoner of Hope.* New Haven: Yale University Press.

Burghardt, S. 1982. *The Other Side of Organizing: The Personal Dilemmas and Political Demands of Daily Practice.* (Chapter 3: Broadening the use of self: Steps toward tactical self-awareness). Massachusetts: Schenkman Publishing Company.

Cain, R. 1993. Community-based AIDS services: Formalization and depoliticization. *International Journal of Health Services.*

Cameron, D. 1994. Debt politics. *Canadian Forum.* Vol.LIXXIV:no.835 (December, p.4).

Camp, D. 1998. Me, Conrad and Hacksaw Al. *Toronto Daily Star.* June 21:F3.

Carniol, B. 1995. *Case Critical (3rd Ed.).* Toronto: Between the Lines Press.

Checkoway, B. 1995. Six models of community. *Community Development Journal.* Vol.30:no.1 (pp.2-19).

Colorado, P. and D. Collins. 1987. Western scientific colonialism and the re-emergence of Native science. *Practice: the Journal of Politics, Economics, Psychology, Sociology, and Culture.* Winter:pp.51-65.

Cruikshank, J. 1990. The outsider: An uneasy role in community development. *Canadian Social Work Review.* vol.7:no.2 (pp. 245-259).

Cruikshank, J. 1989. Burnout: An issue among Canadian community development workers. *Community Development Journal.* Vol.24:no.1 (pp.40-54).

Dale, D. 1978. *How to Make Citizen Involvement work.* University of Massachusetts: Citizen Involvement Training Project.

Dale, D. and N. Mitiguy. 1978. *Planning for a Change.* University of Massachusetts: Citizen Involvement Project.

Desroches, L. 1996. *Allow the Water.* Toronto: editions DUNAMISpublishers.

Edmunds, R.D. 1984. *Tecumseh and the Quest for Indian Leadership.* Boston: Little Brown.

Ehrenreich, B. 1993. They call it democracy: "The worst years of our lives". *This Magazine.* Vol.27:no.3 (pp.12-15).

Entourage. 1989. Insecure incomes (summary of a report of the G. Allan Roeher Institute). Vol.4:no.2 (spring, pp.3-7).

Erlich, J.L. and F.G. Rivera. 1995. *Community Organizing in a Diverse Society (2nd ed.).* Toronto: Allyn and Bacon.

Fals-Borda, O. and M.A. Rahman. 1991. *Action and Knowledge.* London: Intermediate Technology Publications.

Finks, P.D. 1984. *The Radical Vision of Saul Alinsky.* New York: Paulist Press.

Forcese, D. 1975. *The Canadian Class Structure.* Toronto: McGraw-Hill Ryerson Ltd.

Freire, P. 1970. *Pedagogy of the Oppressed.* New York: Seabury Press.

Fromm, E.. - 1966. *You Shall Be As Gods.* New York: Fawcett Premier.
  - 1964. *The Heart of Man.* New York: Harper and Row.
  - 1961. *Marx's Concept of Man.* New York: Fredrick Ungar publishing Co.
  - 1955. *The Sane Society.* New York: Fawcett Premier.

Gallagher, A. 1977. Women and community work. In M. Mayo (ed.), *Women In the Community.* (pp. 121-144). London: Routledge and Keegan Paul Ltd..

Gandhi, M.K. 1951. *Non-violent Resistance.* New York: Sihocken Books.

Gastil, J. 1993. *Democracy in Small Groups.* Philadelphia: New Society Publishers.

Germain, C. and A. Gitterman. 1980. *The Life Model of Social Work Practice.* New York: Columbia University Press.

Gilroy, J. 1990. Social work and the women's movement. In B. Warf (ed.), *Social Work and Social Change in Canada.* Toronto: McClelland and Stewart.

Hall, E.T. and M. Reed Hall. 1987. *Hidden Differences.* New York: Doubleday.

Hope, A. and S. Timmel. 1984. *Training for Transformation.* (Vol. 1-3). Gweru, Zimbabwe: Mambo Press.

Horwitt, S.D. 1989. *Let Them Call Me Rebel.* New York: Alfred A. Knopf.

Howe, N. and P. Longman. 1992. The next new deal. *The Atlantic.* vol.26:no.4 (April, pp. 88-99).

Illich, I.. 1972. *Deschooling Society.* New York: Harper and Row.

Jeffries, D. 1993. *Community Development and Aging: A Case Study of Conflict Resolution in a Seniors' Housing Co-op.* Gerontology Development Project: School of Social Work, McMaster University.

Joreen. 1973. The tyranny of structuralessness. In A. Kordet et al. (eds.), *Radical Feminism.* New York: Quadrangle.

Kahn, S. 1994. *How People Get Power.* Silver Springs, MD: NASW Press.

Kahn, S. 1982. *Organizing.* New York: McGraw-Hill.

Kerr, S. 1993. A tale of two cities: review of Peter Skerry 1993, "Mexican Americans: The ambivalent minority". *The New York Review of Books.* Vol.XL:no.21 (p.3).

Kieffer, C.H. 1984. "Citizen empowerment: A developmental perspective." In Rappaport, J. and R. Hess eds. *Studies in Empowerment Groups: Towards Understanding and Action.* New York: Haworth Press

Kramer, R.M. 1970. *Community Development in Israel and the Netherlands.* (Research series No. 14). Berkley, California: University of California Institute of International Studies.

Kretzman, J.P. and J.L. McKnight. 1993. *Building Communities From the Inside Out.* Chicago ACTA Publications.

Kuyak, J. 1991. *Fighting for Hope.* Montreal: Black Rose books.

Laidlaw, A. F. 1961. *The Campus and the Community: The Global Impact of the Antigonish Movement.* Montreal: Harvest House.

Lakey, G. 1987. *Powerful Peacemaking.* Philadelphia: New Society Publishers.

Lakey, B. et al. 1995. *Grassroots and Nonprofit Leadership.* Philadelphia: New Society Publishers.

Langer, E.J. 1983. *The Psychology of Control.* Beverly Hills: Sage Publications.

Laxer, J. and A. Martin. 1976. *The Big Tough Expensive Job.* Montreal: Press Porcepic.

Learner, M. 1979. Surplus powerlessness. *Canadian Social Policy.* Jan./Feb.:pp.18-27.

Lee, B. 1998. *Advocacy: Contexts, Principles, and Practice.* Mississauga: CommonAct.
   - 1992. Colonialism and community. *Community Development Journal.* Vol.27:no.3   (pp.211-219).
   - 1988. *Purpose and Meaning in Community Development.* Unpublished Doctoral   Thesis, Ontario Institute for Studies in Education.

Lee, B. and M. Balkwill. 1996. *Participatory Planning for Action.* Mississauga: CommonAct Press.

Lee, B., S. McGrath, U. George and K. Moffat. 1996. Community practice education in Canadian schools of social work. *Canadian Social Work Review.* Vol.13:no.2 (pp.221-235).

Lee, C. 1993. Big Cove suicides find relief in healing week. *Beedaudjimowin.* Vol.13:no.2 (October, pp.23,29,38).

Levy, J. 1985. *Cesar Chavez: Autobiography of la Causa.* New York: W.W. Norton and Company Inc..

Lotz, J. 1995. The beginning of community development. In B. Wharf and M. Clague (eds.), *Community Organizing: Canadian Experiences.* Toronto: Oxford University Press.

Macpherson, C.B.. 1977. *The Life and Times of Liberal Democracy.* Toronto: Oxford University press.

Maier, N. 1961. *Frustration.* Ann Arbor: University of Michigan Press.

Maier, N. and P. Ellen. 1965. The integrative value of concepts. In R. Lawson (ed.), *Frustration Theory.* New York: MacMillan.

Matthiesson, P. 1992. *Indian Country.* New York: Viking Press.

Mayo, M. 1977. Community development for social change. In R. Bailey and M. Brake (eds.), *Radical Social Work.* Pp. 129-143. London: Edward Arnold.

McDermott, P. 1992. Employment equity and pay equity: And never the twain shall meet. *Canadian Women Studies.* Vol.12:no.3 (spring, pp.24-27).

McFarlane, P. 1993. *Brotherhood to Nationhood: George Manuel and the Making of the Modern Indian Movement.* Toronto: Between the Lines Press.

McGrath, S. 1998. *The Politics of Truth: A Case Study by the Social Planning Council of Metropolitan Toronto: 1957-1988.* PhD. Thesis: University of Toronto.

McGregor, R. 1990. *Chief.* New York: Viking Press.

McKnight, J. 1995. *The Careless Society: Community and Its Counterfeits.* New York: BasicBooks.

McQuaig, L. 1998. *The Cult of Impotence.* Toronto: Penguin Books.

Mowbray, M. 1985. The medicinal properties of localism. In R. Thorpe and J. Petruchenia (eds.), *Community Work or Social Change?* London: Routledge and Keegan Paul.

Moyer, B. 1990. The Practical Strategist (Monograph). San Francisco: Social Movement Empowerment Projects.
   - 1987. The Movement Action Plan (Monograph). Philadelphia: Movement for a new Society.

Mulally, B. 1997. *Structural Social Work (2nd. Ed.).* Toronto: Oxford University Press.

Narayan, U. 1994. Working together across differences. In B.R. Compton and B. Galloway (eds.), *Social Work Processes (5th ed.).* (Pp.177-188). Pacific Grove, Calif.: Brooks/Cole Publishing Company.

National Round Table on Aboriginal Urban Issues. 1993. *Royal Commission on Aboriginal Peoples.* Ottawa: Minister of Supply and Services.

New Yorker, The. 1989. The Talk of the Town. June 26:pp.25-29.

Obonsawin, A. 1993. *Kanehsatake: 270 Years of Resistance.* (Film). Ottawa: National Film Board of Canada .

O'Malley, K. 1998. Grassroots in cyberspace. *Canadian Forum.* Vol. LXXVI:no.866 (Jan/Feb, pp.21,22,27,29).

Omatsu. 1993. In K. Aguiter-San Juan (ed.), *The State of Asian-America's Activism in the 1990's.* Boston: South End Press.

Paton, R. 1994. The need to reform information policies. *Canadian Speeches: Issues of the Day.* April:pp.20-24.

Piven, F. and R.A. Cloward. 1977. *Poor People's Movements.* New York: Pantheon Books.

Playboy Magazine. 1972. Interview with Saul Alinsky. March:pp.59-178.

Ponting, J.R. 1986. Institution building in an Indian community: A case study of Kahnawake. *Arduous Journey: Canadian Indians and Decolonization.* p. 155. Toronto: McClelland and Stewart.

Ravitz, M. 1982. Community development: Challenge of the eighties. *Journal of the Community Devlopment Society.* Vol.13:no.1 (pp.1-2).

Repo, M. 1977. The falacy of "community control". In J. Cowley et al. (eds.), *Community or Class Struggle?* Pp.47-64. London: Stage 1.

Rice, J. 1990. Volunteering to build a stronger community. *Perceptions.* Vol.14:no.4 (autumn, pp.9-16).

Rice, J. and M.J. Prince. 2000 (forthcoming). *Changing Politics of Canadian Social Policy.*

Reinharz, S. 1992. *Feminist Methods in Social Research.* (Chapter 10: Feminist Action Research). New York: Oxford University Press.

Rifkin, J. 1998. God in a labcoat. *Utne Reader.* May/June: pp.66, 106-108 - 1995. *The End of Work.* New York: G.P. Putnam's Sons.

Ristock, J.L. and J. Penell. 1996 *Community Research as Empowerment.* New York: Oxford University Press.

Roberts, H. 1979. *Community Development Learning and Action.* Toronto: University of Toronto Press.

Romero, P. 1987. *E. Sylvia Pankhurst: Portrait of a Radical.* New Haven: Yale University Press.

Ross, D. et al. 1994. *Canadian Factbook on Poverty - 1994.* Ottawa: Canadian Council on Social Development.

Ross, M.G. 1972. *Community Organization (2nd. Ed.).* New York: Harper and Row.

Rothman, J. and J. Tropman. 1987. Three models of community organization and macro practice perspective: their mixing and phasing. In F.M. Cox et al. (eds.), *Strategies of Community Organization (3rd ed.).* Itasca, Illinois: F.E. Peacock Publishers.

Rubin, R.J. and I. Rubin. 1986. *Community Organizaton and Development.* Toronto: Merrill Publishing.

Russell, B. 1977(1918). *Roads to Freedom.* London: Unwin Paperbacks.

Rykert, L. and M. James 1998. *Working Together Online.* Toronto: Metastrategies Inc.

Saul, J. Ralston. 1995. *The Unconscious Civilization.* Toronto: Anansi.

Sennett, R. And J. Cobb. 1972. *The Hidden Injuries of Class.* New York: Vintage Books.

Sharpe, G. 1973. *The Politics of Non-violent Action (vol.1-3).* Boston: Porter Sargent Publishers.

Shields, K. 1994. *In the Tiger's Mouth.* Philadelphia: New Society Publishers.

Skidmore, R.A. and M.G. Thackery. 1976. *Introduction to Social Work.* Englewood Cliffs, New Jersey: Prentice-Hall Inc..

Specht, H. 1969. Disruptive tactics. In R.M. Kramer and H. Specht (eds.), *Readings in Community Organization Practice*. Pp.372-386. New Jersey: Prentice-Hall Inc..

Speck, R.U. and C.L. Attneave. 1973. *Family Networks*. New York: Pantheon.

Speeter, G. 1978. *Power: a Repossession Manual*. University of Massachusetts: Citizen Involvement Training Project.

Staples, L. 1984. *Roots to Power*. New York: Praeger Special Studies.

Stinson, A. 1979. North Frontenac community services: Case study of a rural community service. In B. Warf (ed.), *Community Work in Canada*. Pp.87-1128. Toronto: McClelland and Stewart Limited.

Strean, H.S. 1979. Role theory. In F. Turner (ed.), *Social Work Treatment (2nd ed.)*. New York: Free Press.

Suzuki, D. 1995. Why the U.S. is a dismal model for us. *Toronto Daily Star*. Dec. 2:C5.

Swift, J. and B. Tomlinson. 1991. *Conflicts of Interest and the Third World*. Toronto: Between the Lines Press.

Thomas, D.N. 1983. Participation in politics and the community. In D.N. Thomas (ed.), *The Making of Community Work*. London: George Allen and Unwin.

Tremain, R. 1973. *The Fight for Freedom for Women*. New York: Ballantine Books.

Wadsworth, Y. 1984. *Do it Yourself Research*. Melbourne: Victorian Council of Social Services.

Wagamese, R. 1996. *That Terrible Summer*. Toronto: Warwick Publishing.

Warren R.L. 1983. Observations on the state of community theory. In R. Warren and L. Lyon (eds.), *New Perspectives on the American Community.* Homewood, Ill.: Dorey Press.
- 1977. Organizing a community survey. In F. M. Cox et al. (eds.), *Tactics and Techniques of Community Practice.* Pp.23-35. Illinois: F.E. Peacock Publishers.

Webster, P. 1997. Open sesame. *This Magazine.* July/August:pp.13-15.

Weeks, W. 1994. *Women Working Together: Lessons from Feminist Women's Services.* Cheshire: Longman.

Wharf, B. ed - 1992. *Community and Social Policy in Canada.* Toronto: McClelland & Stewart
- 1990 *Social Work and Social Change in Canada.* Toronto: McClelland & Stewart.

Wharf, B. and M. Clague, eds. 1997. *Community Organizing: Canadian Experiences.* Toronto: Oxford University Press.

White, R.W. 1959. Motivation reconsidered: The concept of competence. *Psychological Review.* 65:5-197.

Whitmore, E. and P. Kerans. 1988. Participation, empowerment and welfare. *Canadian Review of Social Policy.* Issue #22.

World Development Report. 1997. *The State in a Changing World.* Washington: World Bank.

Wycoff, H. 1980. *Solving Problems Together.* New York: Grove Press.

If you are interested in re-ordering this, or any other books published by CommonAct Press, please call or fax us at (416) 410-3770 (the number will take both faxes and phone calls). We will be happy to answer any of your questions. You can also reach us via our web page www.commonact.com or at our email address info@commonact.com

Name: _____

Occupation: _____

Organization: _____

Address: _____

_____

Telephone: _____ Fax: _____

Email: _____

Please indicate how many copies of each you would like:

Pragmatics of Community Organization ($19.95)_____

Participatory Planning for Action ($9.95) _____

I would like a desk copy of the 3rd edition of Pragmatics for review _____

I would like to be put on your mailing list
to find out about other upcoming publications _____

We've Moved To:
CommonAct Press
7050 Old Mill Lane,
Mississauga, ON
L5W 1A1, Canada
telephone and fax number: (416) 410-3770
e-mail: info@commonact.com
web site: www.commonact.com